SHADY LADIES

SHADY LADIES

*Nineteen Surprising
and Rebellious American Women*

SUZANN LEDBETTER

A TOM DOHERTY ASSOCIATES BOOK NEW YORK

Book design by Nicole de las Heras

A Forge Book
Published by Tom Doherty Associates, LLC
175 Fifth Avenue
New York, NY 10010

www.tor.com

Forge® is a registered trademark of Tom Doherty Associates, LLC.

ISBN-13: 978-0-765-30827-6
ISBN-10: 0-765-30827-4

2005033714

First Edition: August 2006

Printed in the United States of America

0 9 8 7 6 5 4 3 2 1

CONTENTS

ACKNOWLEDGMENTS

Enormous gratitude is extended to Pat LoBrutto, a most patient man and editor extraordinaire, who took this idea for a book and told me to run with it, and to Paul Stevens, senior editor. Robin Rue, the world's best literary agent, sealed the deal, as she has in my behalf for a decade.

Not only did Paul W. Johns voluntarily plunge into preliminary research on this project, but he delivered his notes in a binder, as well. With the subjects divided in alphabetical order. And all sources annotated. *Wow* doesn't begin to express my appreciation. What word or string of them possibly could?

Jim Veatch, technical services librarian for the Thomas Branigan Memorial Library in Las Cruces, New Mexico, photocopied and shipped to my doorstep information I'd spent months trying to locate, and did so within five days of my desperation SOS e-mail—including a weekend. Jim's wife, Justine Honeyman, assisted in that warp-speed answer to a prayer. There will, at some near-future date, be margaritas all round 'neath a stellar New Mexican sky.

Dave Ellingsworth, my hero, adored husband, business manager, and crack proofreader, fact- and photograph-finder, provided everything I needed during the writing process, be it a critical piece of the historic puzzle, encouragement, support, a meal, or a bottomless cuppa joe.

Gratitude is also given to the Springfield–Greene County (Missouri) Library System for speedily processing numerous interlibrary loan requests, and to the libraries that generously responded: Lawrence University Library, Ellis Library (UM-C), Eden-Webster Library System, West Linn Public Library, Miller Nichols Library (UM-KC).

Add to those, research and photo/illustration-support suppliers: Dick and Sue Hart Wheeler, Zachary J. Ledbetter, the Library of Congress, University of Oklahoma Press, Arizona Historical Society, Denver Public Library, Colorado Historical Society, University of Texas-Austin Center for American History, Chicago Historical Society, Oregon Historical Society, and the Yukon Archives.

And last, but by no means least, thanks be and God bless to every author of every book, publication, newspaper article, Internet source, and diarist listed in the bibliography. Someone once asked me how many books it takes to write a book. The answer is multi-paged and contained at the back of this one.

INTRODUCTION

I have bursts of being a lady, but it doesn't last long.

—SHELLEY WINTERS

"So," I've been asked repeatedly, "what *is* a shady lady?" The question, I might add, is typically accompanied by one of those winks, nudges, or crimped eyebrows commonly described in fiction as *knowing*.

The implication that my authentic cast of characters is wholly of the soiled-dove persuasion isn't entirely incorrect. A few were, truth be told, or managed a business devoted to plying the world's oldest profession. Yet even they possessed a je ne sais quoi that distinguished them from your basic bride of the multitudes.

However their keep was earned, these ladies' brand of shadiness was more akin to nonconformity than moral turpitude—which, in their heydays, was pretty much the same thing.

Fanny Fern had the audacity to write the truth as she lived, felt, and observed it, a century before Betty Friedan's *Feminine Mystique* was deemed "revolutionary."

Harriet Hubbard Ayer's beauty-oriented newspaper column might appear frivolous by comparison, but in 1896, touting cosmetic "artifices" was tantamount to turning half the population into rouged, face-powdered trollops. That Ms. Ayer owned a cosmetic factory wasn't a coincidence, but the vernacular lacked a term for her meld of advertising and editorial content until *advertorial* entered the dictionary in 1946.

Frances Johnston wielded a camera for a female's-eye view of the world in all its ironies. Her visual pursuit of the truth as she saw it included students in an impoverished, reservation Indian School debating whether Negroes in the South should be granted full citizenship.

Against all odds and detractors, Bethenia Owens-Adair qualified to become a Doctor of Medicine at a time when the majority of male sawbones hung out their shingles with impunity and no practical training whatsoever.

Which isn't to say every Shady Lady's motive was honorable, let alone selfless. One of them could have vied for the title Queen of Mean. Noble or not, they prevailed despite criticism, ostracism, public and private defamation, and in some instances, imprisonment and grinding poverty.

Why these women in particular intrigued me enough to research their life stories poses another question lacking a pat answer. A partial explanation involves a rabid fascination with rebels, especially female rebels, with or without a cause. Add to that, a fondness for dreamers and schemers, especially those who manipulate schemes into the achievement of dreams, regardless of consequences.

With one exception, these women also possessed a sly sense of humor. The one reputed never to have cracked a smile was so dour, her antics read like punch lines to politically incorrect jokes.

I'll grant, if a proverbial, resurrection-style dinner party were possible, I'd be a conversational spectator, not a participant. Come to think of it, a series of teas for two would better fit the bill. Particularly since at least two on the full guest list might be packing heat. And Wilma Minor accompanied by her mother and spirit guides portends a houseful right there.

A commonality all these women possess is a fall to relative obscurity; in the case of Margaret Brown, an enduring fable slanders the accomplished woman she was.

For all our foremothers whose names and claims to fame survive and are revered, reviled, or reiterated in countless college theses and dissertations, there are hundreds, if not thousands, whose deeds, be they semi-dastardly, or humbling, should ne'er be forgot.

Of those, I present my personal-favorite nineteen and sincerely hope you enjoy making their acquaintance.

Suzann Ledbetter

SHADY LADIES

(Oregon Historical Society, #OrHi 4062)

I

BETHENIA OWENS-ADAIR

*You will change your mind when I come back a physician,
and charge you more than I ever have for your hats and bonnets.*

The phrase *mad as a hatter* derived from the addlepating
(often fatal) side effects of the nitrate of mercury haber-
dashers once employed to shape and stiffen felt. In 1870, Bethenia Owens's family questioned her sanity when she announced
her intention to shutter her successful millinery shop and study
medicine.

As word of Bethenia's lunatic ambition spread through
Roseburg, Oregon, a respected female friend confided that
she'd never "submit" to a woman doctor. If the woman explained why she preferred a male doctor, the reasoning was
never elucidated. It surely stemmed from gender bias rather
than common sense, as less than a fourth of frontier doctors in
those days actually held degrees from accredited colleges. The
rest either apprenticed themselves to formally, or equally un-

formally, trained physicians, were self-taught by means their patients were probably better off remaining ignorant of, or simply tacked DOCTOR on a shingle in front of their Christian names and slapped it upside their office door.

Bethenia was wounded by the criticism and dearth of support, but had already overcome enough hardships in her then thirty years to feel she'd earned the right to pursue a career in the healing arts. Ironically, her father might have contributed the inspirational impetus and necessary stubborn streak.

"Thomas Owens is not afraid of man or the devil," Bethenia once said of the former Pike County, Kentucky, sheriff, who'd arrived in Oregon Territory in 1843 with a wife and two children and naught but fifty cents in his pocket. Less than a decade of farming the fertile Clatsop plain at the mouth of the Columbia River parlayed Owens's four-bit nest egg into a princely net worth of twenty thousand dollars.

Though a self-proclaimed tomboy, Bethenia was the second eldest of Thomas and Sarah's nine children and the eldest daughter. This virtually preordained her role as "the family nurse, and it was seldom that I had not a child in my arms and more clinging to me. Where there is a baby every two years, there is always no end of nursing to be done. . . ."

That is, when she wasn't engaged in farm chores or feats of strength to impress her older brother. According to *Maverick Women* by Frances Laurence, the petite Miss Owens once bet him she could tote four fifty-pound sacks of flour at once. Ever the gentleman, as he graciously loaded the sacks onto her back and under her arms, he was likely divining how he'd spend such easy money—after, of course, he rescued his boastful sister flattened in the dirt beneath two hundred pounds of flour.

Bethenia won the bet and probably several others, yet as the adage goes, sometimes when you win, you lose. Her mother vocally and often disparaged her unladylike daughter's shenanigans. When a former farmhand named Legrand Hill asked Thomas Owens's permission to wed then fourteen-year-old Bethenia, Sarah seconded the approval and quite possibly sighed with relief.

Lest contemporary readers be appalled by the Owenses' blessing, both boys and girls in their midteens were considered to be adults. Life expectancies were short, families large, and children expected to pull their own weight, practically as soon as they could walk upright.

That Legrand Hill's assets consisted of twenty dollars in cash, a horse and saddle, and a rifle didn't concern Bethenia one whit. "I thought my husband was the equal of any man living," she said.

Chalk it up to love's reputed blinding effect, or a heavy helping of wishful thinking. Before their son George was born in 1856, it was clear that Legrand preferred hunting, reading, and get-rich-quick schemes to anything that smacked of manual labor. Their first year together, Bethenia despaired that winter was coming on, yet the cabin Legrand had started months earlier was still absent a floor and a roof.

Pride and the sterner stuff she was made of might have induced her to endure her loafer-husband's lack of ambition, but she would not tolerate the abuse he began leveling at their son.

Childbirth had left Bethenia ill and weak, and the baby was sickly and often fretful. Legrand spanked the child for crying. Bethenia intervened, only to be struck and choked for trying to protect her son. The day Legrand threw the baby on the bed and stormed out in a rage, Bethenia packed her and George's meager possessions and moved back to her parents' farm.

"I was never born to be struck by mortal man," she said—a statement personalized and elaborated upon when her hot-tempered husband begged for a reconciliation. "I have told you many times that if we ever did separate, I would never go back, and I never will."

Filing for divorce triggered an ugly court battle with her mother-in-law for custody of George. Bethenia prevailed on all counts and won the right to revert to her maiden name, as though it would expunge all memory of the hellish three years she'd spent as Mrs. Legrand Hill.

Loath to accept charity, which is what she deemed the financial assistance her family offered, Bethenia took in laundry and ironing, sewed, picked berries, and hired out as a nurse and housekeeper to support herself and her little boy.

Between her numerous jobs and mothering a small child, one would think she'd have scant time to sleep, yet Bethenia wasn't content "because of my intense thirst for learning. An education I must have at whatever cost."

The price exacted was the humiliation of a twenty-year-old functionally illiterate single mother attending a one-room schoolhouse and "reciting with children from eight to fourteen years of age."

Friends often found her studying a propped-up book while ironing or laundering other people's clothes for the pennies it paid. Reflecting on those grueling years, she said,

> No more is it necessary for the student to pore over the old, thumb-worn books by the light of a pitch stick, or a tow string

in a broken mug of refuse kitchen grease; and yet those times produced from and for this nation a Franklin, a Jefferson, a Greeley, a Clay, a Webster, and a Lincoln . . . who possessed the sterling qualities of intelligent, incorruptible citizenship . . .

In 1861, her diligence and persistence reaped a steadier income when she qualified for a teaching certificate—unusual for an era when schoolmarms were commonly required to be spinsters, which technically, Miss Owens was not.

The roof over her and George's heads, she provided with the four hundred dollars she'd saved to build a tidy cottage in Astoria, Oregon. As Gayle C. Shirley relates in *More Than Petticoats: Remarkable Oregon Women*, "[Bethenia] . . . judged herself now to be ready to take on the world."

Centuries before, Horace observed in his *Epistles*, "As soon as a man perceives how much the things he has discarded excel those which he pursues, let him return in time, and resume those which he relinquished." That was precisely Legrand Hill's intention when he appeared on Bethenia's "cozy little porch."

Since the divorce, Hill had written her any number of letters, apologizing for his abusive behavior, promising he'd never raise his voice or hand to her or their son again, pleading with her to remarry him.

"But alas for him," Bethenia wrote in her memoirs. "He found not the young, ignorant, inexperienced child-mother whom he had neglected and misused, but a full-grown, self-reliant woman who could look upon him only with pity."

She did grant Hill the equivalent of visitation rights, but was wise and wary enough to inform the sheriff of the arrangement, fearing her former husband might try to smuggle George out of town.

At her parents' urging and to further her now twelve-year-old son's education, Bethenia moved back to Roseburg to profit on her sewing ability by opening the town's only dress and millinery shop. Exclusivity being the handmaiden of supply and demand, for two years, she eked out what passed as a living, until a competitor stole away her customers and declared Bethenia to be "a rotten hat designer and an even worse businesswoman."

Vitriol notwithstanding, Bethenia agreed. Armed with a $250 bank loan, she decamped to San Francisco for a short course in professional millinery design. Upon her return to Roseburg, she leased a storefront across the street from her sharp-tongued rival. The ensuing (albeit fickle) female stampede to Bethenia's door netted a $1,500 profit within the first year.

In 1870, two unrelated life-changing events propelled her toward a secret yet longheld dream. While her business was flourishing, George's departure for the University of California at Berkeley left her nest empty in ways designing fashionable chapeaus and voraciously reading medical textbooks couldn't fill. Providence intervened when a friend, aware of Bethenia's nursing skills, summoned her to treat her seriously ill child.

Bethenia arrived to witness the local sawbones's (a probable graduate of the hang-out-a-shingle school of medicine) umpteenth attempt to insert a catheter in his small, screaming patient. Frustrated, he laid down the instrument to wipe his spectacles.

Bethenia pounced. In seconds, she accomplished the procedure, bringing immediate relief to the tortured child. Rather than thank Bethenia for her assistance, the ham-fisted physician lambasted her for interfering.

Instead of putting her in her place, the experience galvanized Bethenia's passion to earn a medical degree. Within days, she was memorizing a borrowed copy of *Gray's Anatomy* in preparation for her enrollment at Philadelphia's Eclectic School of Medicine.

By her own admission, it wasn't a particularly revered institution. The curriculum centered on hydropathy, that is, the treatment of diseases via medicinal baths. Eclectic, to be sure, if not outright quackery, but it was also one of the few medical colleges that accepted female applicants.

In addition to her classwork, Bethenia attended lectures at Philadelphia's Blockly Hospital and employed a private tutor to broaden her knowledge of the healing arts. A year later, duly certified as a "bath doctor," Bethenia visited Roseburg en route to Portland, where she intended to base her practice.

Whether as a dare, a practical joke, or an attempt to shame Bethenia publicly, Roseburg's medical community sent an invitation to the "Philadelphia doctor" to attend a derelict's autopsy. They expected her to decline, like a proper lady most certainly would.

The fifty or so men and boys crowding the shed where the postmortem was to be performed fell back to allow the lady doctor's entrance. An excerpt in Gayle C. Shirley's, *More Than Petticoats* reiterates Bethenia's description of the other six doctors' reactions:

. . . I shook hands with Dr. Hoover, who advanced to meet me and said, "The operation is to be on the genital organs." I answered, "One part of the body should be as sacred to a physician as another. Doctor Palmer [of the ham-fisted catheterization procedure] stepped back and said, "I object to a woman being present at a male autopsy. If she is allowed to remain, I will retire."

As even a casual acquaintance of Dr. Bethenia Owens would foresee, she hesitated not a second in calling the bluff in a haughty yet thoroughly professional manner. Reminding Palmer of the written invitation she'd received, she then asked him to explain the difference between a woman attending a male's postmortem and a man witnessing a woman's.

Her request for a vote to decide whether she should stay or leave resulted in a five-to-one approval of her participation. Defeated and infuriated, Palmer stalked out of the shed, but the bath doctor's "hazing" was far from over. One of the yea-sayers offered her his instruments, snidely challenging her to perform the dissection.

By the time Bethenia finished, Roseburg was abuzz with the news of her disgusting, scandalous behavior. She later remarked that if not for her brothers' reputed proficiency with firearms, she might well have been tarred, feathered, and run out of town on the proverbial rail.

Either the gossip grapevine didn't stretch the 240-some miles to Portland, or its citizens ignored the distant whispers. Women and children queued up at Dr. Owens's office door, eager to pay $1.50 each for a soothing medicinal soak. Among them was the rival milliner who'd insulted Bethenia's hatmaking and business acumen.

In response to the woman's apology for her viciousness and request for medical treatment, Bethenia said, "Once a friend told me, if I wished to increase your height, I'd attempt to press you down. You'd grow from sheer resentment. So I thank you for your rudeness, for it made me grow."

As did her practice. Prosperity allowed Bethenia to pay George's tuition to the Medical Department at Willamette University and her younger sister's college education. She also honored a female patient's deathbed wish to adopt the eldest of her three daughters.

The forlorn little girl, Mattie Bell, was underfed, undersized, and dressed in rags when her father delivered her to her new foster mother's home. Years later, a friend Bethenia had once asked to buy Mattie some decent clothes stopped by and said, "What did you ever do with that little girl you took, when I was here last?"

Mattie emerged, now sixteen and the picture of health and happiness. Though she later married and established a home of her own, Mattie's devotion to her adopted mother remained constant. When Mattie died in her early thirties, Bethenia's grief was tempered by her daughter's knowledge that her birthmother loved her enough to give her a stable home and that Bethenia had loved her like her own child.

Ever the pragmatist, Bethenia later wrote, "I have done my duty to those depending on me, and now I will treat myself to a full medical course, and a trip to Europe. I shall then be equipped for business on a grand scale."

Again, her family believed she'd taken leave of her senses. Closing a successful medical practice, her bank accounts, and selling her property was . . . well, essentially the same thing Thomas Owens did back in 1843, when he moved his family from Van Buren County, Missouri, and hit the Oregon Trail. If Bethenia wasted any breath to that effect, the point was likely neither welcomed nor taken.

As it had during her tenure as the oldest student in a one-room schoolhouse and her training at the Eclectic School of Medicine, her regimen of cold baths, little sleep, and daily exercise served her well.

> During all that time I had not suffered from a day's sickness and had been present at every class lecture save one, my absence from it being due to my having been so deeply absorbed in my studies that I failed to hear the bell. This lapse almost broke my heart, which had been set on being able to say, at the end of the course, that I had not missed a single lecture.

When she returned to Portland in 1881, the forty-one-year-old "bath doctor" had earned a bona fide M.D. from the esteemed University of Michigan—a "mixed" school she'd have applied to a decade earlier, had she known the institution accepted female students.

Her area of specialty was diseases of the ear and eye. Her practice thrived, not inconsequentially due to her opinion that "no one expects to get a prescription for less than $2.00." A belief perhaps instilled by her son, George, now in the pharmaceutical business in Goldendale, Washington. Bethenia had long considered herself wed to her profession. The perpetual tomboy nonconformist had taken to the ice on skates, kept gossips' tongues a-wag by riding horses astride, and despite (or maybe to spite) her years as a milliner, went about in blissful, bareheaded rebellion. Independent in word, deed, and spirit, she'd have laughed uproariously had someone predicted she'd fall instantly in love with a handsome, charming, articulate widower.

Colonel John Adair was a West Point graduate, a farmer, land developer, and no stranger to Bethenia, though she'd been a mere child when he became the first collector of customs in Astoria—later, its first postmaster.

He made no secret of his boundless admiration and affection for Bethenia, which she returned in kind. Their courtship was brief, culminating in marriage on July 24, 1884.

Their joy at the birth of a daughter in 1887 changed to overwhelming grief when the infant died three days later—a tragedy from which Bethenia never fully recovered. It's hardly speculation to presume that for all her medical training and prowess, her inability to save Mattie Bell or her baby girl would haunt Bethenia for the rest of her days.

She and John did eventually raise Mattie's son, Victor, and adopted another deceased patient's newborn son, whom they named John Adair Jr.

Well before then, however, it was evident that Bethenia had married another occupational bon vivant. John's military background and prior positions did not a profession make. Like Legrand Hill, he was a sucker for fast-talking schemers and deals too good to be true.

The circular pattern of much of Bethenia's life was completed when she relocated the family and her medical practice to an isolated farm near Astoria: a far remove from con artists' beaten paths, yet ostensibly to ease Bethenia's developing and painful rheumatism.

Of the shift from a specialized city practice to general rural one, she wrote,

> I carried on my professional work as best I could in that out-of-the-way place; at no time did I ever refuse a call, day or night, rain or shine. I was often compelled to go on foot, through trails so overhung with dense undergrowth and obstructed with logs and roots, that a horse and rider could not get past; and through muddy and flooded tide-lands in gum boots.

As this was by no means an appropriate geographic prescription for muscles, joints, and fibrous tissue already inflamed with rheumatism, shortly before the turn of the century, she and John moved to North Yakima, Washington. The climate there was somewhat drier, and George was, as Bethenia had long hoped, practicing medicine in that city.

Closing her gladstone bag for the last time October 1905, Bethenia returned to the family farm in Astoria. Retirement not a facet of Bethenia's vocabulary, she commenced a tireless one-woman campaign to secure voting rights for women. She also wrote legislation mandating prenuptial medical examinations and advocated the sterilization for the mentally incompetent and criminally insane.

An excerpt of one of her published essays, reproduced in *Maverick Women,* by Frances Laurence, leaves no doubt about Dr. Owens-Adair's viewpoint on the subject:

The greatest curse of the race comes through our vicious and criminal classes, and to my mind this is the element that should be dealt with . . . by the science of surgery, for if their power to reproduce themselves were rendered null, a tremendous important step in advance would have been taken.

Both bills passed into Oregon state law before Bethenia succumbed to inflammatory heart disease on September 11, 1926. John Adair, her adored but exasperating husband, had preceded her in death eleven years earlier.

Bethenia Owens-Adair wasn't the first woman to graduate from medical school. That honor belongs to Dr. Elizabeth Blackwell, who in 1849 received her degree after completing the then-required thirty-two-week course.

It's safe to say, however, that few, if any, women ever worked as hard or long, or battled as much opposition from as many directions for the right to scribe *M.D.* after her name.

A flat, poorly tended cement marker identified Dr. Owens-Adair's grave until a group of Clatsop County, Oregon, residents banded together and erected a proper stone in July 1975. The engraving reads: "Only the enterprising and the brave are actuated to become pioneers."

(Chicago Historical Society, ICHi-19640)

2

HARRIET HUBBARD AYER

When I say that no woman need be obese, no woman,
if she have not an organic disease, need be bony, no woman need
grow bent and haggard and yellow, faded or wrinkled; I assert
what I have proved not once, but thousands of times.

—FROM ORIGINAL PREFACE,
HARRIET HUBBARD AYER'S BOOK:
A COMPLETE TREATISE
ON THE LAWS OF HEALTH AND BEAUTY

Harriet Hubbard Ayer's life story is stranger than fiction, for unlike real life, fiction must make sense to engage and retain a reader's suspension of disbelief.

In the case of Mrs. Ayer, a credible explanation for the extent and viciousness of the conspiracy to destroy her professionally, physically, and mentally defies comprehension, even a century after the fact.

Born in Chicago on June 27, 1849, Harriet was only four

when her father died of pneumonia. When news of his death reached his wife, Juliet, she lived up to her Shakespearean namesake by declaring herself ready to die, as well.

Her sisters disabused her of the notion by volunteering to caretake their nephew, Henry, and nieces Juliet (Jule), Harriet, and eleven-month-old May, freeing the wealthy widow to assuage her grief in Paris.

Upon her return, she insisted upon henceforth and forevermore being addressed as *Madame* Hubbard. She retained the title both during and after a brief marriage to a traveling poet, whose face and name none of her children could later recall.

Harriet, the third-youngest, "the plain, uninteresting one," was afraid of her own shadow and terrified of the dark, thus bore the brunt of her older siblings' teasing and Madame's criticism.

Just past her fifteenth birthday, Harriet attracted attention of a different type and source: the ardor of Herbert Crawford Ayer, son of Chicago iron magnate, John V. Ayer—a son the senior Ayer wasn't aware he had, until the previous year.

The Chicago press had made a cause célèbre of John's chance encounter with his ex- (and supposedly deceased first) wife and their grown son. As the story went, the couple had eloped after a few hours' acquaintanceship. Unaware she was pregnant, the bride deserted John, filed for divorce, then sent a messenger saying she'd succumbed to yellow fever.

Although John had long since remarried and fathered three children, he declared prodigal son Herbert the heir to the ironworks business, relegating younger son and namesake, John Jr., to hereditary second banana.

One needn't be prescient to view the marriage of Harriet Hubbard—the shy, naive ugly-duckling daughter of an aloof, self-centered mother—and Herbert Ayer—the skirt-chasing, whiskey-guzzling, instantly wealthy son of an industrialist—as not of the made-in-heaven variety.

Harriet tried her best to be the perfect wife. In the end, accomplishing that goal was her downfall.

Two pregnancies fraught with excruciating headaches and insomnia produced daughters Harriet (Hattie) and Gertrude (Gert). At first sight, Herbert was besotted with Hattie, but Gert was asthmatic, fretful, and, worse, not of the male persuasion.

Equally displeasing to Herbert was his wife's appearance. It's said that a woman marries expecting her husband to change, and a man marries believing his wife will not. If so, Harriet and Herbert were equally disappointed.

Pregnancy didn't agree with Harriet physically, but outwardly, the meek, ugly duckling had blossomed into a stunning, chestnut-haired swan. As for Herbert, neither leopards nor Victorian party animals change their spots. Marriage and fatherhood didn't affect his wee-hours carousing one iota.

On the night of Sunday, October 8, 1871, he was, as usual, absent the house, when Nora, the Ayers' maid, alerted Harriet to the approaching wall of flames she'd seen from the nursery's window.

Herbert arrived as the two women rushed from the house with Hattie and Gert. They joined the mob clogging the street, frantic to escape the hellish fire and thick, acrid smoke.

Dawn was breaking before they reached the safety of John V. Ayer's south-side mansion—hours too late for baby Gert's fragile lungs and heart. Harriet refused to believe her baby was dead. She had to be sedated with morphine to remove the infant from her arms.

Come Tuesday, while rain soaked the charred aftermath of

the Great Chicago fire, Harriet Ayer, numb with grief, locked herself in a room and sewed obsessively for the destitute—her meticulous stitches one of the few practical skills learned during her brief attendance at Sacred Heart Academy.

According to *The Three Lives of Harriet Hubbard Ayer,* her mother-in-law took a small embroidered dress off the stack and gave it back to Harriet. "Save it for your next baby. You are young. Wounds heal. Think how lucky you are to be alive, the two of you. And you have little Hattie."

After Harriet's death, the dress was found tucked inside a box of treasured mementos.

The fire spared Mme. Hubbard's house, but cholera and smallpox plagued the city. She refuged to Paris, a reluctant Harriet and granddaughter Hattie in tow.

French couturier M. Worth's special interest in the beautiful Mrs. Ayer broke every current fashion rule: He insisted her hair be skimmed back from her face, with loose curls at the brow and a simple knot of curls at the nape. The original Greek-inspired gowns he designed complimented Harriet's figure (and those of few others).

A French tutor was hired for herself and Hattie. Harriet also attended plays, where during intermission, she memorized theater-goers' varied accents, mannerisms and body language. She read voraciously and eclectically—art history, poetry, medical books, Parisian cooking and cuisine, architecture and design—whatever struck her fancy.

Long daily walks relaxed her and lessened her chronic insomnia (a possible side effect of nyctophobia). One afternoon, she happened upon a small chemist's shop. While she watched the proprietor formulate a violet-scented perfume specially for her, he mentioned that somewhere in his cluttered laboratory was a recipe for skin cream used by Napoleonic beauty, Mme. Recamier.

He allowed that Harriet's flawless complexion needed no such treatment, but he'd look for the formula, in the event she someday returned to France and wanted a jar.

Back in Chicago, the new house was nearing completion. The reluctance Harriet felt when she left the city assailed her on the return trip, yet letters she'd received from Herbert saying how much he loved and missed her and Hattie renewed hope for a fresh start—a second chance to salvage their marriage.

Herbert met the ship in New York City. Harriet's glide down the gangplank clad in Worth from hat to toe drew dozens of admiring eyes . . . and a glower from her husband.

To his way of thinking, his wife had cheated him out of a year of his beloved daughter's life, and Harriet's newfound aura of sophistication and culture was evident to everyone, save her. Herbert's wealth and standing in the Chicago business community weren't self-made, but at the behest of his father. Now Harriet, the child-woman Herbert had wed and expected to hover in his slender shadow, cast a wider, deeper one. Adding insult to injury, little Hattie spoke with a slight French accent.

Over the next few years, Harriet's every effort to please him, to ingratiate herself with Chicago's social elite, often had the opposite effect. "I felt," she later wrote, "that if I stopped even for one second, something terrible would happen. It was as though I were on fire and running from myself."

Her charitable work and patronage of and passion for the arts was roundly admired and respected (Herbert, of course, excepted), but also provided an escape from an increasingly unhappy home.

Following several miscarriages, Harriet gave birth to another daughter, Margaret. Herbert's displeasure was eclipsed by the death of his father; his grief at becoming sole owner of Ayer & Company was as transparent as isinglass.

His megalomania, alcoholism, serial adultery, and jealous, increasingly violent rages became intolerable. Harriet packed up her two daughters and decamped to New York City, where Mme. Hubbard now lived.

Within months she received word that Herbert had sold the house and contents to stave off bankruptcy. Harriet's friend, Mrs. Lyon, had salvaged and stored what possessions she could: "small pieces, bric-a-brac, crystal and china."

On February 17, 1883, newspaper headlines read A TOTAL COLLAPSE—THE FAILURE OF JOHN V. AYER'S SONS DECLARED TO BE ABSOLUTE AND SWEEPING—misplacing equal blame for the company's mismanagement on Herbert and the brother he'd superseded.

Given Harriet's eternal identification with and compassion for the underdog, a genuinely contrite, humbled Herbert might have rewon her heart. Instead, like an aging pugilist, he alluded to a better-than-ever "come back," but admitted, "I didn't mean us to end this way. You are welcome to the divorce any time, if you can pay the lawyers."

Quite the magnanimous exit line, considering Harriet, who'd never held a job in her life, must support herself, Hattie, and Margaret, as Mme. Hubbard's lifestyle had severely dented her deceased husband's estate.

Because most employers believed a woman's place was in the

home, job opportunities were scarce, low-paying, and menial. A secondary conviction held that a female's physical and intellectual inferiority justified lower wages for the same job.

Domestic service and the sewing trades constituted traditional "women's work." An experienced sewer, for example, was paid by the piece and averaged twelve-hour days to meet the most basic monthly living expenses.

Harriet quickly realized that her greatest asset was her social standing: she was as well known in New York's elite circle as in her native Chicago. Syper & Company, an exclusive purveyor of European antiques, home furnishings, and decor items hired her as a commissioned salesclerk. Within a week, she'd sold merchandise equivalent to a full year's salary.

Success afforded a brownstone on West Thirteenth Street, which did double duty as "Artistic Furnishings & Shopping," a private showroom for Syper's wealthiest clients. Harriet's long hours and European buying trips added a governess and a housekeeper named Lena Raymond to the all-female household.

A hefty commission earned from decorating oilman "Arizona Jim" Seymour's new yacht allowed Harriet to make now fourteen-year-old Hattie's dream a reality: studying music at a conservatory and finishing school in Stuttgart, Germany.

The school, owned by popular novelist and accomplished pianist Blanche Willis Howard, was recommended by a trusted friend, whose daughter would also attend that fall. Under Miss Howard's charismatic tutelage, students studied world affairs and cuisine, art, music, literature, as well as how to create and manage a home to perfection.

A few weeks before Hattie's departure, Jim Seymour invited her, Margaret, and Harriet to the yacht's christening, in keeping with his oft-stated policy of never breaking a promise or forgetting a slight.

Harriet was aware that the married multimillionaire's interest in her extended beyond her flair for design. His subtle advances reaped naught but gentle rebuffs, yet she was intrigued by his business acumen. She agreed, the road to riches wasn't paved by commission sales. Except thinking big on borrowed money, as he advised, was precisely what had bankrupted her estranged husband.

Seymour also heartily approved of his son Lewis's infatuation with Hattie. To Harriet's relief, the interest didn't appear mutual. Twenty-year-old Lewis Seymour was a decent young chap, but his minimal education and cultural exposure did not a prospective husband make (an assessment similar to Mme. Hubbard's, when Herbert Ayer came a-courting).

By fall, an ocean separated Hattie from her eager suitor, along with her mother and sister. To Harriet's aggravation, Hattie was a better pianist than a correspondent. The same wasn't true of Blanche Howard. With each letter Harriet received, her trust and affection for her daughter's mentor deepened. Blanche often expressed awe for Harriet's single-handed raising of a daughter as talented and charming as Hattie. Her sincerity and fondness for Hattie moved Harriet to tears.

While on a buying trip for Sypher's, Harriet visited the school and confided to Blanche her concerns about Margaret. The nuns at the convent school Margaret attended frequently remarked on her inability to sit still for long, her refusal to learn to read, her mischievous behavior.

Harriet blamed herself—the long hours she worked, the insomnia it provoked, the morphine powder she resorted to when exhaustion pushed her to the brink of collapse. Herbert was a forerunner to a deadbeat Disneyland dad, his visits erratic, his train fare and armloads of gifts bought on credit, but never a thin dime for his daughters' tuition, clothes, or—heaven forbid—Harriet's rent.

Blanche understood, sympathized, called Harriet "her heroine," and offered to take Margaret under her wing. Hattie missed her little sister and would set a most marvelous example for Margaret, and vocal training would enhance the girl's natural singing ability.

Harriet lived for her children. Being separated from both of them for much of the year was inconceivable. And, from a practical standpoint, musically gifted or not, she couldn't afford double tuition.

"That's why you must be brave," was Blanche's reported reply. "It is not the children who owe their parents a great debt. You and I know it is the parents who owe the debt to the children they brought into the world. They didn't ask to be born . . ."

The best is all any parent wants for a child, regardless of the sacrifice, be it financial or emotional. For Harriet, the best she could give her daughters was Blanche Howard's tutelage. What she didn't know—couldn't in her wildest imaginings have foreseen—was the horrific price all three of them would eventually pay.

While in Paris, the last leg of her buying trip, Harriet returned to the chemist's shop whose proprietor had created her now-trademark violet perfume. A week later, having purchased the formula for Mme. Recamier's skin cream, the brownstone's kitchen became a makeshift laboratory.

With housekeeper Lena Raymond's willing assistance, Harriet worked night after night, experimenting, improving on the formula, refining, testing, and then perfecting a lightly violet-scented salve that brought back the roses to even a chronic insomniac's cheeks.

Her second guinea pig, Mme. Hubbard, was aghast at the very idea of applying maquillage (makeup). Such products were the purview of kept women, prostitutes, dance-hall floozies, foreigners, and the generally déclassé.

Not that proper, self-respecting ladies were above a dab of vegetable rouge, or dissolving sulphate of iron in gum water and brushing the semitoxic concoction on their eyebrows and lashes. Victorians of both sexes, having raised a sort of blithe hypocrisy to an art form, believed it one thing to mix and apply "artifices" in the privacy of one's boudoir, and quite another to purchase them ready-made—much less admit needing them.

As satirized in a Max Beerbohm essay, a husband who suspected his wife's loveliness was not entirely God-given, ". . . bade her sternly, 'Go up and take it all off,' and on her reappearance, bade her with increasing sternness, 'Go up and put it all on again.'"

Thus when Mme. Hubbard asked her daughter for more cream, Harriet sensed she had a gold mine in a blue china jar. A handshake agreement was reached with Jim Seymour to borrow fifty thousand dollars in exchange for five hundred shares in her enterprise as collateral.

Over time, her relationship with the oil tycoon had evolved to a platonic friendship. Admittedly having no head for business, she bowed to his judgment that the cream should retail for $1.50 per jar.

Harriet Hubbard Ayer had been rich and she'd been poor. Rich was infinitely better, but she wasn't about to count profits before they materialized. By day, she ran her home-based Artistic Furnishings & Shopping. At night, she oversaw the Harriet Hubbard Ayer, Inc., factory on Sixth Avenue and its offices on Park Place.

By name, the Recamier brand lent a coveted Francophilian cachet (read snob appeal) to the skin enhancer and rejuvenator. To capitalize, Harriet's advertorials feted Mme. Julie Recamier as the most beautiful woman in France for over forty years, about whom Napoléon allegedly said, "I fear Madame Recamier's influence against me more than the muskets of a whole army."

Testimonials from the Princess of Wales, Sarah Bernhardt, Lillian Russell, and Lily Langtry credited the cream with remedying everything from freckles and blotchiness to blackheads—thereby giving cosmetics a very public stamp of approval.

Harriet may not have originated advertising's "before and after" illustrations, but the picture-worth-a-thousand-words idea was enormously effective. Of course, the company's elegant, strikingly beautiful founder was the ultimate testimonial. Recamier Products quickly became a household name from coast to coast and across Europe.

Beauty tips and advice in brochures she wrote actually tied appearance to self-confidence as much as or more so than the use of cosmetics. Later in book form, she said, "I believe that good women can be more helpful, more uplifting, and wield a stronger moral influence if they are lovely to look at, graceful as well as gracious, perpetually young and beautiful, than the reverse." And, a tad more bluntly,

The woman who has so much to do would never think of neglecting to scrub her floor, or polish her tin pans. . . . But she has no time to take a daily bath, to keep her hair lustrous and well dressed and to preserve her teeth even and white. Instead she allows herself to degenerate into a household drudge and dowd.

Suffragettes were appalled, accusing Harriet of being a traitor to the cause. Rather than embarrass, the vitriol incensed her. Perhaps Harriet agreed with some planks of the feminist platform, but she retorted,

> I am always a bit amused when anathemas are hurled at the present use of cosmetics, particularly when a hopelessly-soured and pitilessly-unattractive female or a blatant, tobacco-smoking, spirituously-odorous male addresses me on the subject.

Orders and profits rolled in. The Recamier line expanded to balms, soaps, face powder, hair products, depilatory, and tonics. On the family front, now in Stuttgart with Hattie, Margaret was excelling in her studies and vocal training.

Although Harriet's home-furnishings business assistant, Lottie Mason, became her corporate office assistant, Harriet worked as many hours and slept as little as ever. And Jim Seymour was not content to be a silent partner. His constant, unwelcome intrusions forced Harriet to remand critical information to a mental file cabinet and she locked any papers in a closet at home.

Wills clashed—personally and professionally—when Hattie announced her intention to marry Lewis Seymour, a long-distance courtship of which Arizona Jim and Blanche Howard were aware, but one kept secret from Harriet.

Vowing to repay Seymour's still-outstanding loan immediately, she called at his Wall Street office in the hope he'd agree that for similar reasons, a Seymour–Ayer marriage was as doomed to fail as hers and Herbert Ayer's.

She never disclosed exactly what happened behind that closed office door. By piecing together clues, it's apparent she rejected his amorous advances, stated flatly her noninterest in becoming his mistress, and likely issued choice words aplenty regarding his son sharing the same planet as her daughter, let alone becoming her husband.

Whatever Seymour's definition of "a slight" deemed unforgettable, Harriet exceeded it. He ranted to an office boy, "I'll make her pay, if it's the last thing I ever do."

Events spanning the next five years of Harriet's life would seem exaggerated—if not completely fabricated—save a wealth of evidence and corroborating documentation.

The first hint of trouble came as New Yorkers dug out from the Blizzard of '88. Mme. Recamier's Park Place office was in chaos—orders stockpiled, shipments delayed so long, their recipients canceled them altogether. When questioned, Lottie Mason said she was following Jim Seymour's instructions. She was fired on the spot.

Clerical duties were added to Harriet's already leviathan workload. Her plan to bring Margaret home for the summer (in truth, permanently) ended with a letter from Blanche saying the girl had contracted scarlet fever. While packing to board the next ship bound for Germany to be with her sick child, Harriet collapsed from exhaustion.

As children are wont to do, Margaret's recovery was speedy and complete. Her mother was hospitalized for months, leaving rested but scarcely rejuvenated.

Hattie and Lewis's November wedding at Harriet's brownstone portended an enormous strain. She'd repaid Seymour's loan, but his presence, plus Herbert Ayer's, attending on Jim Seymour's nickel, fostered thoughts of a hen hostessing a fox convention in her own coop.

A transatlantic round-trip to fetch Margaret was beyond Harriet's endurance. In a letter to her daughter, Harriet expressed her regrets and promised, after the ceremony, she and Lena Raymond (now a dear friend more than a housekeeper) would come to Stuttgart and bring Margaret home for good.

Forewarned of Harriet's intentions, Blanche Howard secretly cabled Jim Seymour: "Treatment begins December 26." How and when they conspired to destroy Harriet is unclear. Bizarre though it sounds, their equally pathological motivations meshed perfectly.

Blanche's was twofold and began the moment Margaret Ayer had become her pupil: Test the effectiveness of mind-control techniques by systematically brainwashing Margaret into believing her mother was an incurable alcoholic or morphine addict or both. If successful, Margaret would become the de facto daughter Blanche couldn't have.

Hattie Ayer was already Mrs. Lewis Seymour, living at the family enclave in East Orange. What sweeter revenge could Jim Seymour exact on Harriet than to finance Blanche's plot to take Margaret away from her, too?

The "treatment" to which Blanche alluded began within hours of Harriet and Lena's arrival at the Stuttgart school. Starting with the first cup of cocoa Blanche served, Harriet's drinks were laced with sulfonal. Marketed as "the reliable hypnotic," in small doses, the heroin derivative acted as a light sedative. In large, persistent doses, the effect was cumulative and toxic, causing extreme lethargy, mental impairment, and repressed respiration. Visible side effects included dry, grayish-sallow skin, unfocused vision, and "inelastic" muscles.

Within days, Harriet was virtually comatose. Lena, playing the role of obsequious, illiterate Negro maid, rendered herself invisible to Blanche. Soon realizing how Harriet was being drugged and why, Lena substituted drinks mixed with pow-dered chalk for those containing sulfonal.

Plot foiled, Blanche enlisted a confederate to whisk Mar-garet from the house, then ordered Harriet and Lena to leave immediately. Knowing the Stuttgart police would never believe them over the esteemed Blanche Willis Howard, Harriet and Lena had no choice but to return to New York.

A CRIME ALMOST INCREDIBLE IN THIS CENTURY, is how the *New York Herald* portrayed the conspiracy and theft charges Harriet levied in civil court against Jim Seymour on May 20, 1899. He'd not only abetted Howard's character assassination and murder attempt, but while Harriet was in Germany, he'd stolen paperwork locked in her brownstone's closet: the cipher code to the Recamier formula and letters proving she'd repaid the loan to assert half-ownership of Harriet Hubbard Ayer, Inc.

Seymour appeared bored by the proceedings. When the judge disallowed letters from Margaret to Hattie (coerced, if not scripted by Blanche Howard), accusing Harriet of every-thing from nipping hair dye to mouthwash, Seymour gave them to the press, who printed them in their odious entirety. Sleaze tactics aside, Stephen Olin, Harriet's attorney, presented sufficient evidence and corroborating testimony to convince Judge Daly to find for Harriet Hubbard Ayer.

Why criminal charges were never brought against Seymour,

Blanche Howard, and a bevy of accomplices is unknown, but the evil, transatlantic chess game had only begun.

Harriet also triumphed over Lottie Frenzel's (née Mason) claim to thirty shares of stock. Frenzel then filed suit, alleging *she'd* invented the Recamier cream and Harriet had reneged on the guaranteed, five-thousand-dollar annual salary as payment for the formula.

A week after the court found again in Harriet's favor, Herbert Ayer (induced and bankrolled by Jim Seymour) filed for custody of Margaret to keep Harriet from taking her away from Blanche Howard.

Herbert testified that his now ex-wife frequently entertained men in her home and was an alcoholic and morphine addict. Combined with Margaret's infamous letters, libelous screeds from Blanche Howard, a deposition from Lottie Mason Frenzel, and testimony solicited via Seymour's checkbook regarding Harriet wandering the street "clad only in blue tights," the court granted Herbert's petition.

As stated in *The Three Lives of Harriet Hubbard Ayer*,

> Jim Seymour knew then what some people are still in process of discovering: that accusations against a moral character or integrity of a person are remembered long after the individual in question has been completely cleared. Therefore, in order to damage a reputation, it is not necessary to have either facts or evidence; all that is needed is no regard for the truth, no conscience and an outlet to the public.

Manipulating and alienating both of Harriet's daughters (as well as her sisters, Jule and May), the heartbreak of watching

Mme. Hubbard die from cancer, nearly destroying the business Harriet worked to exhaustion to build—none was punishment enough to satisfy Jim Seymour.

On February 9, 1893, in accordance with a petition signed two days earlier by Herbert Ayer and Hattie Ayer Seymour and bribes paid to Dr. J. W. Morton, Harriet Hubbard was committed to a private insane asylum in Bronxville, New York.

To awaken from a drugged stupor in a dank, shuttered cell would frighten anyone. It was terrifying beyond comprehension for a woman so fearful of the dark that the walls of her homes were always painted pale pink and the lights dimmed, but never extinguished.

In time, the dress and undergarments she wore that night fell to tatters. Her shoelaces rotted through; she begged attendants for bits of string to knot together. Twice a month, she was permitted to bathe, then redressed in the same fetid clothes. Her hair turned gray and matted for want of a comb or brush. Books were prohibited, including the Bible, but she was allowed to mend sheets by the flicker of a kerosene lantern.

Letters she wrote were opened, then destroyed. Any mailed to her were intercepted. No one, other than family members, could visit. None did.

Another inmate, a Freemason (whose identity she never disclosed) told her in French that because he'd committed himself, he had special privileges and could post letters for her. By then, Harriet wouldn't trust the Angel Gabriel if he alighted on her cot. She had naught more to lose, yet daren't hope attorney Stephen Olin would receive her letter.

On April 8, 1894, the New York State Commission of Lunacy adjudged that Harriet Hubbard Ayer was sane. Their decision wasn't reached via patient interviews, an examination, or psychiatric evaluation, but was based on a legal technicality. Dr. J. W. Morton, who'd certified Harriet's insanity in February of the previous year, was not lawfully qualified as an Examiner in Lunacy, until the day *after* he signed the commitment order.

Harriet left the asylum wearing what remained of the clothing she wore the night she arrived. She had lost over forty pounds, and the bedraggled dress hung on her like a macabre Halloween costume. Even wearing a double-set of colored glasses, Harriet found sunlight tortured her nearly blind eyes, accustomed to darkness. Frail and bowed of back, her once-flawless complexion faded to ghostly gray, the legendary beauty William Chase captured in two oil paintings resembled an aged crone. She was forty-four years old.

Whatever the cream of Chicago society that packed Central Music Hall on April 15, 1896, expected for the price of admission, Harriet Hubbard Ayer delivered a hundredfold.

She glided across the stage dressed in a gorgeous white evening gown. Her gray hair was cropped short with ringlets framing her face, and her weight precisely the 136 pounds her Recamier brochures recommended for a woman five feet four inches tall. The milky cast to her eyes had vanished and, with it, so had her eyeglasses.

"Fourteen Months in a Madhouse" was the title of her lecture. She began by saying that whatever their motives, she held no malice toward anyone responsible for her commitment. Her sole intent was to garner support for amending laws to protect the rights of the insane and allegedly insane alike.

Midway through the presentation, she changed into her ragged dress and string-bound shoes. The curls were brushed from her hair. When she returned to the stage, she appeared shrunken, fragile, and decades older.

The effect, coupled with the description of the degradation, deprivation, and abuses she'd endured, was at once horrifying and mesmerizing. For the finale, she redonned her evening gown, adding the Masonic pin given her by her anonymous savior. She held up the certificate that ordered those fourteen months in a madhouse, then the one that set her free to illustrate that sanity and insanity were too often determined by signatures on sheets of paper.

Did she defeat her enemies or simply outlast them? A bit of both, it seems.

When she told lecture audiences she felt no ill will toward anyone who'd harmed her, it wasn't to cast herself as a martyr, a saint, or a victim. She meant every word.

Margaret eventually extricated herself from Blanche Howard's clutches. Harriet's understanding and love for the daughter lost to her for eight years absolved Margaret's guilt and diminished the psychological and emotional damage Howard had inflicted.

Even before Arizona Jim Seymour cashed in his dwindling net worth, abandoned his wife and family, and skedaddled to California, Hattie realized her father-in-law made Machiavelli look like an amateur. For Harriet, the past was meaningless; being reunited with both her daughters was all that mattered.

The forgiveness extended to Herbert Ayer. He was penniless and mortally ill, but however he'd wronged Harriet, he would always be Hattie and Margaret's father. Harriet paid for his transport from Chicago to New York, a rented room, and nursing care, so his daughters could be with him at the end.

While at Bronxville, Harriet's personal property, real estate, and jewelry were sold to pay the asylum's fees and keep Harriet Hubbard Ayer, Inc., afloat. Thanks to years of negative publicity and absent its founder, the company was hemorrhaging red ink. Its namesake had neither the stamina nor means to revive it, but knew what interested women, as she told *New York World* Sunday editor, Arthur Brisbane.

The beauty advice column she pitched was a bona fide overnight success. Her byline soon frequented the *Evening World*, as well, and reader mail poured into the newsroom by the bagful.

In 1899, *Harriet Hubbard Ayer's Book: A Complete and Authentic Treatise on the Laws of Health and Beauty* was a bestseller. In its preface, she wrote

> I most sincerely hope and believe that every woman who does me the honor of reading what I have to say will find many hints and suggestions that will be useful to her and to others whose welfare she has at heart—for it is my earnest wish to be of practical service.

As a reporter, Harriet was tireless, indefatigably curious, and the consummate professional. While *World* colleague Nellie Bly became synonymous with "stunt" or "detective" journalism, the subjects of Harriet's features ranged from destitute tenement dwellers to a First Lady to a convicted murderess serving a life sentence in a London prison.

On Sunday, November 19, 1903, Harriet wakened with a cold. She'd covered a horse show the evening before and worked late to compose the story and have it messengered to the newspaper for the evening edition.

By Tuesday, the doctor Margaret summoned diagnosed pneumonia—along with influenza, the leading cause of death before the advent of penicillin. For the next two days, Hattie and Margaret never left their mother's bedside, caring for her, comforting her, trying to rally her fighting spirit.

As Margaret's biography recalled, on the morning of Thursday, November 23, Hattie whispered in her mother's ear, "You are going to get well, my dearest, I feel it."

Harriet smiled at her, said, "You are a sweet little faker," and breathed her last.

Her funeral service was attended in equal number by the city's poorest and its most prominent citizens. The flag atop the *New York World* building was lowered to half-mast.

"For a woman?" one reporter asked. To which Don Seitz, the newspaper's business manager, shot back, "She was the best man on the staff."

Four years later, Vincent B. Thomas bought the rights to and trademarked Harriet Hubbard Ayer's signature Recamier product line and formulas. For a time, the company became a rib of the (Unilever) Lever Bros. umbrella.

Harriet Hubbard Ayer's Book, reprinted in 1974 by The New York Times Book Company, is described by one reviewer as "a charming addition to any beauty professional's library, along with enthusiasts and writers of romance novels."

A tube of Reganne pink lipstick by Harriet Hubbard Ayer was included in the inventory of the John F. Kennedy and Jacqueline Kennedy Onassis Memorabilia Collection, auctioned by Hantman's in July 2003.

(Yukon Archives, Collection: Munger Family fonds, 78/112 #4)

3

MARTHA MUNGER BLACK

My first thrill of freedom came with my marriage,
when at last, unchaperoned, I could go to the Vienna Bakery,
a place with a naughty reputation.

Taken out of context, the above sounds as though Martha Louise Munger had been confined to a convent during her formative years. In actuality, her parents did transfer their daughter to St. Mary's of Notre Dame, a convent school renowned for discipline, after Martha's abbreviated stint at Lake Forest Select Seminary for Young Ladies.

In her autobiograpy, *My Seventy Years,** she acknowledged that she wasn't disobedient or disrespectful. Her "zest for adventure" triggered a sort of temporary amnesia concerning rules and regulations.

---

*Edited by Flo Whyard and reissued in 1976, as *Martha Black, Her Story from the Dawson Gold Fields to the Halls of Parliament.*

By 1898, that irrepressible zeal would have her "speeding northward to the Klondyke, where, that winter, all alone in a little cabin of that grim north country, I was to face the darkest hours of my life . . ."

A life that began approximately thirty-two years earlier, although when and where depends on the source. A photograph of Martha's headstone in Flo Whyard's book reads *Born in Kansas, 1865*, but the caption states, ". . . should have read Mercer, Pennsylvania, 1866."

Compounding the confusion is an excerpt from the autobiography's first chapter: "She [Black's mother, Susan] uttered no complaint about going to Chicago, and here in February 1866 my twin sister and I, Martha Louise Munger, were born."

Martha goes on to say, "I never knew my twin sister as she lived only a few hours. Many times I have longed for her, have imagined the good times we might have had together, the companionship, the unity of understanding, the love that is the heritage of twins."

Susan Munger bore and buried four children before giving her husband, George, a son and heir, as well as another daughter. Meanwhile, their firstborn proved to be, in the vernacular of the day, "a ringtailed tooter."

Martha credited her paternal grandfather, Lyman Munger, with "an intuitive knowledge of child psychology"—a knack vividly employed on the occasion of Martha's fourteenth birthday.

An uncle's gift of a pair of diamond earrings met with not only maternal disapproval, but Susan Munger adamantly refused her daughter's pleas to have her ears pierced, so she could wear them. Grandfather Munger intervened by supposedly taking Martha's side and volunteering to pierce the girl's ears himself.

When the agreed-upon, fateful Saturday arrived, his granddaughter's unbridled glee fizzled fast as she surveyed the equipment he'd assembled for the procedure: a threaded, three-cornered sail needle, a wooden mallet, a log, and a square of linen overlaid with a piece of leather.

Munger explained that he'd rub Martha's earlobe until it was numb, position it on the linen-clad log, whack the needle with the mallet to force it through her lobe and into the leather, then pull the threaded needle through the hole.

Suffice it to say, Martha suddenly remembered a skating party she'd been invited to that afternoon. Procrastination fueled by the family's casual remarks about ear-piercings gone hideously, if not fatally, wrong led to the pinpoint diamond studs' reincarnation as a brooch.

Her father's influence was as much an aggravation as an inspiration to Martha. After the Great Chicago Fire destroyed the Munger home and George's prosperous laundry, he rebuilt both, expanding his business to a chain of seventy-two laundries, nationwide. Other far-flung ventures included a sugar plantation in the West Indies and a two-thousand-acre ranch in Kansas. Managing those interests required constant travel, yet he found time to share his fascination with higher mathematics with Martha.

Other than the terminology, the intricacies of calculus to binomial theorem were eventually lost to her, but botany became a lifelong hobby. She recalled once telling her father that she could find a hundred four-leaf clovers without taxing herself unduly.

Thinking he'd tamp her flair for braggadocio, George promised a dollar for every one she found. "Before the end of the second day," she wrote, "I had gathered over 50. Father paid me the money and asked to be released from his bargain, declaring he had enough good luck to last all the rest of his life."

How home-schooling in advanced mathematics and challenging her eagle eye for flora factored into George's lofty ambition for both his daughters falls a bit shy of comprehension, but he often said,

> Someday one of my girls may be the wife of the President of the United States and live in the White House, and I want her to know how to fill a position like that. On the other hand, one of my girls may have to work for the President's wife, and I want her to know how to do that equally well.

It must have gone without Martha's repeating that his aspiration for George Jr. was to capture the Oval Office. Being several years younger than Martha, perhaps his presidential term was to piggyback her someday spouse's.

Fate played a different hand. Martha became neither First Lady nor her personal secretary. The House she'd occupy at the age of seventy wasn't addressed 1600 Pennsylvania Avenue; in fact, it wasn't on American soil. However, if one puts stock in a palmist's foresight, her journey from increasingly dissatisfied Chicago housewife, society matron, and mother of two sons to a seat in the Canadian Parliament was predestined.

An appointed audience with Count de Hamong, aka Cheiro, brought Martha to a darkened room where the seer, dressed in a voluminous purple robe, was seated at a table. Whether the palm reader was a good guesser, or genuinely prescient, he told his skeptical guest, "You are leaving this country within the year. You will travel far. You will face danger, privation, and sorrow. Although you are going to a foreign land, you will be among English-speaking people, and will never have to learn to speak another language. You will have another child, a girl, or an unusually devoted son."

Martha dismissed the prediction, yet it rekindled that long-fallow zest for adventure. Her ten-year marriage to Will Purdy, her teenaged sweetheart, was feeling like slow suffocation. When news of a mother lode gold strike in the Canadian Yukon reached the Lower 48, it seemed like a cure for their ailing relationship.

Purdy's lucrative position as a railroad paymaster afforded his wife and sons, Warren and Donald, a lovely home and servants, but the job required constant travel. Martha tried filling the void of an absent spouse with her now school-aged children, freelance writing, charitable functions, club work, the theater, card parties, and parlor games, but was, quite frankly, bored to the bone.

And she was hardly alone in that pre–turn of the century restlessness. As Richard O'Connor related in *High Jinks on the Klondike*, "Agitation for women's suffrage and abolition of the double standard was reaching its crescendo, and the moral superiority of women was dinned into men's ears with merciless reiteration."

The fairer sex's escalating uppityness, a heavy contributor to the much-mourned taming of the West, along with a rickety national economy, the unionization movement and accompanying riots and the Cuban Rebellion of 1895 set the tone for, as O'Connor aptly described, ". . . a fight, or a frolic."

The military-minded repaired south to wrest Cuba from Spanish control. A far larger army of what O'Connor called "congenital optimists" rushed north to Dawson, Canada, to claim a share of the Yukon bonanza.

If commonalities existed among the Klondike stampeders, they were acute naïveté and pure ignorance of the region many couldn't have located on a map—before *or* after they arrived. Guidebooks were published as fast as presses could print them, which, for the value of the information purveyed and a match, a gold-fevered argonaut could tender a small fire.

Among the wholly unprepared onslaught were Will and Martha Purdy, whose sons were left in the care of her parents on their Kansas ranch. Also up for a frolic were Martha's brother, George, and friends Eli and Sophy Gage. With funds provided by Purdy's and Gage's fathers, Will and Eli had formed the Purdy-Gage Company and bought two oceangoing tugs, a steamer, and two sailing vessels.

Prospects of a great Canadian adventure aside, Martha's enthusiasm for the trip skyrocketed when the nephew of a deceased millionaire Klondike prospector named William Lambert approached her father-in-law for assistance in settling Lambert's estate.

In her memoirs she states,

> Father Purdy suggested that this be my special work. The idea was acceptable to all concerned, and the proper papers were drawn up. Father Purdy insisted that I should receive a 50 per cent division of the gold dust, half a million dollars, and if I did not survive this hazardous undertaking, that it should be made over to my children.

The arrangement raises questions Martha doesn't address: For instance, why did her father-in-law charge her with this "hazardous undertaking," rather than his son, Will? Naming their sons Warren and Donald as Martha's primary beneficiaries seems a trifle odd, too, unless the elder Purdy feared both the boys' parents might perish. If so, it's difficult to imagine why he helped bankroll the expedition.

Whatever the motivation, before the Purdys sailed from Seattle, Will received a telegram from the Gages, summoning him to San Francisco for a final business meeting. A week later, Will wrote Martha, waiting impatiently in Seattle. He admitted to sudden reservations about the Klondike excursion and said he'd heard fortunes were being made in the Sandwich (now Hawaiian) Islands. Would she consider going there? Or better yet, go home until Will decided between an Arctic summer's extreme brevity and year-round tropical breezes.

"Go to the Sandwich Islands? With my Klondyke ticket bought, my passage booked, my vision of a million dollars in gold dust? Even after 10 years of married life how little Will Purdy knew me!"

Her brother George balked at her decision to continue northward, sans husband. Not surprisingly, Martha prevailed.

"I wrote to Will that I had made up my mind . . . that I would never go back to him, undependable as he had proven, that I never wanted to hear from or see him again."

This "Dear Will" missive could be construed as a threat and ultimatum to get Will off his supposed cowardly duff, back to Seattle, and aboard ship. If so, it failed, for Martha added, "He went his way. I went mine. I never did see Will Purdy again. He died years later in Honolulu."

Before long, Martha realized a Purdy *had* accompanied her to Dawson, more-or-less just as the palm reader predicted. O'Connor's *High Jinks on the Klondike* so succinctly relates, "Already the mother of two children and carrying her third child . . . she survived the perils of Skagway, the steep assault on Chilkoot Pass and the swirling menace of White Horse Rapids."

Martha's half-million-dollar dreams proved as false as the clapboard storefronts along Dawson's main street. Requisite bribes paid to officials ranging from gold commission officials to postal employees flattened her purse and netted naught but confirmation of the mysterious Mr. Lambert's residence in the Territory. Precisely what had become of him, his will, and the million in gold dust she'd been charged with retrieving was anyone's guess.

The fabulously rich gold mine Martha and George expected to claim didn't materialize as planned, either. Thanks to distance and total isolation wrought by ten-month-long winters, by the time U.S. newspapers trumpeted, GOLD! GOLD! GOLD! GOLD!, prospectors already in the Yukon had staked virtually every square inch of ore-bearing real estate—inches the so-called Bonanza Kings resold to latecomers for thousands of dollars.

Martha and George acquired placer claims along Excelsior Creek—not to be confused with Bonanza Creek, where gold was first discovered—but a little late in the season to sluice much if any ore before winter set in.

Even without Martha's pregnancy, hightailing for home was impossible. She and George arrived in Dawson on August 5. A chart in Tappan Adney's *The Klondike Stampede*, shows that by then, the mercury likely hovered a few ticks above the freezing mark. The mother-to-be had no choice but to make the best of it. A ramshackle cabin almost two miles from the city was turned into a home, and there she handstitched a layette from the linen tablecloths and napkins she'd packed along.

On January 31, 1899, in the midst of the unrelieved darkness of a Yukon winter, Martha gave birth to a nine-pound boy she named Lyman for her beloved grandfather. The birth, she confided decades later to Flo Whyard, was attended by "a one-armed man . . . with a hook for a hand . . . and an old sea captain."

Martha's letter to her parents announcing the birth of her "Little Cheechako" garnered an unexpected result. Just as purple crocus blooms colored the hillsides, her father arrived to escort her back to Kansas and the two older sons she hadn't seen for almost a year.

The stateside reunion was joyous, but within months, homesickness for the north tugged at her, as it did thousands of returning stampeders for whom a "normal" life would forever seem emptier than once it had.

Her father, a world-traveled entrepreneur, must have understood her melancholia more than most, and acknowledged the truth in acorns not falling far from their trees. Diverse investment opportunities were also George Munger's forte. Lastly, whatever his opinion of Martha's marital woes, his unheard-from son-in-law's abandonment of Warren and Donald was unconscionable.

By June 1900, Martha had petitioned for a divorce from Will Purdy and set off for the Klondike accompanied by twelve-year-old Warren. A thirty-acre surface claim (the right to build above ground, not mine below it) was purchased from the Canadian government. When her parents, son Donald, baby Lyman, and a boatload of saw- and quartz-mill machinery arrived the following year, Martha would be ready.

Gold dust was the coin of the Yukon realm, but veins embedded in quartz must be stamped (crushed) mechanically to extract it—an expensive process made dearer by the goldfields' remote location. And, from sluice boxes to buildings and boardwalks, a boomtown's appetite for lumber was insatiable. Like any commodity, demand drove up the price and profits.

Managing a Klondike sawmill was a deviation, if not a paternal concession, for a daughter groomed to become a First Lady (or her right-hand adviser), but Martha and the enterprise thrived . . . until her foreman took exception to her continual chastising about tools being left wherever the workmen cared to drop them.

"I'm sick of being ordered about by a damn skirt, and I'm through," Brockman said.

After "a string of oaths making the air blue," Martha accepted his resignation, only for Brockman to return with the mill's entire workforce, save one. "If you don't take back what you said about us bein' careless of tools and shirkin' on the job, we'll all leave now, and that'll close down your little old tin-pot mill this season."

Like Will Purdy, apparently Brockman wasn't as well acquainted with Martha as he should have been. She fired the whole lot and, well-paying jobs being as scarce as timber to feed the sawmill, replaced the crew within days.

Brockman's continual threats to do her bodily harm compelled her former employees to report him to the Mounties. At their urging, Brockman quit Dawson and Canada altogether, but vowed to "get that hellcat yet."

Martha later heard a sheriff arrested him on outstanding charges the moment he crossed into U.S. jurisdiction.

Excerpts from a chapter in *My Seventy Years* titled "Dawson Settles Down" relates her own contentment.

> . . . there were times of "tough sledding," but there were no tragedies. I had indeed made a new life for myself. I had Donald and Lyman with me . . . Father Purdy had persuaded me to allow him to take full responsibility for Warren and he had now entered him at Annapolis, Maryland.

Martha lived to regret that decision, as Warren never returned to the Yukon.

Prosperity brought an active social life, friendships in arguably the most diverse municipal population on the planet, "plenty of good wholesome fun," and "the most beautiful clothes" to wear to fancy dress carnivals, tea and supper dances, and the annual, ne plus ultra ball hosted by the Arctic Brotherhood.

"Sometimes we women sourdoughs like to boast how popular we were with the men folk," she said, adding,

> . . . in those days we single women, with homes in which to entertain, [a gracious distinction from hurdy-gurdy dancers, prostitutes and consorts] were so few that our number could be counted on the fingers of one hand . . . Scarcely a fortnight passed that I did not have a proposal of marriage.

All of which she declined, until a business appointment with an attorney named George Black eventually decreased Dawson's short roster of eligible ladies by one. "The affairs of human beings move quickly in the North," she said, noting that he'd asked for her hand two weeks after they met. "I was not eager to marry again, yet I liked him more than any man I knew."

Their common interests included politics, botany, ornithology, hunting, fishing and photography, yet George won over her sons Lyman and Donald long before their mother accepted his proposal.

Immediately following their wedding on August 1, 1904, five-year-old Lyman adopted his stepfather's surname, which, upon reaching the age of majority and at Lyman's request, was legalized.

In keeping with her belief that a married couple "should be in complete harmony in religion, in country and in politics," she immediately became "an Anglican, an Imperialist, and a Conservative."

And a staunch supporter of George's burgeoning political career. During an unruly town hall meeting prior to a Yukon Council election, George rose to address the jeering crowd. A woman seated beside Martha said, "They'll never let that man speak!"

Martha replied, "That man will speak if he stands there till hell freezes over. I'm his wife, and I know he won't be scared away by any damn bunch of hoodlums."

Nor would a war half the world away deter by-then Territorial Commissioner George Black from resigning his post in 1916 to form the Yukon Infantry Company.

Among the first to join Captain Black's company was his stepson, Lyman. To Martha's probable relief, Lyman was a year shy of eligibility, but before World War I was over, all three sons were in the military.

Not one to sit by the hearth and roll bandages, Martha ". . . was determined to go overseas on the troopship" with her husband. George's thoughts on the subject were not elucidated, though it can be speculated that he assumed permission would not be granted, thus sparing him the historically established ramifications of saying no to Martha Louise Munger Purdy Black.

Martha repaired to Ottawa to ply her not-inconsequential influence on everyone from the Prime Minister to the Minister of the Marine. To a man, all passed the buck to General Bigger, commanding officer of transportation at Halifax.

"But, Mrs. Black," he reportedly replied to her demand, "you wouldn't want to be the only woman on board a ship with two thousand men, would you?"

"General Bigger, I walked over the Chilkoot Pass with thousands of men and not one wanted to elope with me."

Hours later, after George received his troopship assignment from Biggers, he informed his wife (with a conspicuous lack of enthusiasm), "Well, you can go."

In London, the woman regularly introduced as First Lady of the Yukon, worked for the Prisoners-of-War Department, in the Y.M.C.A. canteen, sewed for the Red Cross and administered the Yukon Comfort fund, visited hospitalized Yukoners, gave lectures on "The Romance of the Klondyke Gold Fields," and became a stringer for the *Dawson News* and the *Whitehorse Star*.

By the time Armistice was declared November 11, 1918,

George was recovering from bullet and shrapnel wounds to both legs, and Lyman had been rewarded with the Military Cross for bravery. To their mother's profound relief, Warren and Donald also survived the war, unscathed.

Following a marginally profitable return to private law practice in Dawson, George was again elected to Parliament, and the couple divided their residence between Ottawa and Dawson. Martha joked that someday her tombstone would read, "She has only moved again." Their semiannual four-thousand-mile journeys from one home to the other also strained the salary of a public servant.

Not a sou had she saved from the profits of the sawmill, stamping company, or placer mines on Excelsior Creek. Like thousands of other prospector-speculators, she had reinvested the money in the constant hunt for that elusive—perhaps mythical—Mother Lode.

Martha's pride at George's election to Speaker of the House of Commons in 1930 turned to concern at reports of his increasingly erratic behavior. A complete nervous breakdown in 1935 necessitated an extended hospitalization and no guarantee of a full recovery.

With the encouragement of numerous supporters, Martha ran as an Independent-Conservative for George's vacated seat. Six years earlier, as the wife of an M.P., she said, during an interview, "The House of Commons sat long this year. I have never been an ardent suffragist, but the longer I live the more I realize that women couldn't do any worse than the 200-odd statesmen that Canada sends to Ottawa each year."

Despite the Liberal Party's otherwise landslide victory, Martha won the opportunity to put that opinion to the test. Though she referred to her election as "keeping the seat warm" for George, it was obviously intended to boost her still-ailing husband's morale, rather than an uncharacteristic fit of modesty.

The seventy-year-old, second-ever female M.P. and now family breadwinner had, as the saying goes, more on her plate than she could say grace over, yet tragedy has the egregious habit of nipping at triumph's heels.

After full days as a Member of Parliament, Martha would work late into the night with coauthor Elizabeth Bailey Price to write her autobiography and choose photographs to include with the manuscripts. Learning her publisher had rejected the project (and kiboshed a magazine serialization deal) marked the first and least of a string of heartbreaking events.

In February 1937, Lyman Black, her "Little Cheechako" was killed in a automobile accident en route to his mother's home in Ottawa. The summer of the same year, her eldest son, Warren, died at the age of forty-eight. Six months later, Martha's brother, George Merrick Munger, passed away at a tuberculosis hospital in Oregon.

Ironically, less than a month after Lyman's death, she told a reporter,

> I wonder if women, for the very reason that they are women, can quite shoulder their full responsibilities in a public manner. Woman's chief mission is not administering artificial respiration to a dying world, nor working perspiringly in a forward movement. Into the life of every woman that is well ordered, come those years of child-bearing and child-rearing. For this reason, most women must defer activity in politics until middle life.

Odd and contradictory as those statements appear, Martha might have been downed by tragedy, but she was far from out. A new publisher released *My Seventy Years* to an enthusiastic readership and generated more lecture invitations than Martha could oblige.

In 1940, her book *Yukon Wild Flowers*, illustrated with George's photographs, was published. The same year, he retook his seat in Parliament, then retired from politics nine years later.

Several falls, then a broken hip confined Martha to a wheelchair. "It's hell to get old," she said, but though it slowed her pace, it didn't cramp her style, or lifelong love of entertaining. "Mr. and Mrs. Yukon's" home, now in Whitehorse, continued to be a mecca for visiting dignitaries, sourdoughs, friends, family members, and writers eager for interviews.

In the process of working on *My Ninety Years*,* a sequel to her earlier autobiography, Martha noted slyly, "The strange, sad history of me life . . . it is a weird one and would be more so if the half could be told."

And never was. When Martha Munger Black died on October 31, 1957, at the age of ninety-one, the Vancouver Province's headline read BRAVE HEART OF THE YUKON FINALLY LETS GO. In accordance with her wishes, her casket was draped with both the Union Jack and the American flag, with officers of the Royal Canadian Mounted Police serving as honor guards.

In time, a Royal Canadian Coast Guard vessel was named

My Ninety Years is contained as an epilogue to Flo Whyard's edited and reissued version of *My Seventy Years*, titled *Martha Black, Her Story from the Dawson Gold Fields to the Halls of Parliament*, published by Alaska Northwest Books.

for her, as was a Yukon mountain (and another for George, her husband of fifty-three years).

Of the woman who seldom took no for an answer and left an indelible mark on two countries, the *Whitehorse Star* said, "Martha Louise Black was the unrivalled queen of all that host of men and women who sought the northern magic . . ."

By her own and others' accounts, Martha found it and reveled in it, till the end of her days.

Fort Brown, Texas, where Sarah Knight Borginnis Bowman became a heroine (Robert Runyon Photographs; E / VN 01887, The Center for American History, The University of Texas at Austin)

4

SARAH KNIGHT
BORGINNIS BOWMAN

*Bring your blankets to my tent tonight and I will learn you
to tie a knot that will satisfy you, I reckon.*

Sarah Borginnis's response to her fiancé's request for a minister to marry them (i.e., tie the knot) was somewhat lacking for romantic. Then again, her betrothed's proposal consisted of answering in the affirmative, when Sarah bellowed, "Who wants a wife with $15,000 and the biggest leg in Mexico?"

Whether the voluptuous Sarah, a laundress and cook during the Mexican War, inflated her net worth or not, her possession of the biggest leg (two, actually) in Mexico wasn't much of a stretch. She stood at least six-two in her stockinged feet and tipped a feed scale at better than two hundred exceedingly top-heavy pounds.

Precious little is known about the first thirty-odd years of

71

Sarah's life. The reported year of her birth varies from 1813 to 1817. Some sources cited her birthplace as Clay County, Missouri, and others listed it as somewhere in Tennessee.

In those days, *vital* hadn't yet attached itself to *statistics*. Nor was it unusual to delay recording a birth in the family Bible, until a newborn's survival seemed reasonably assured. By then, Mom might well be expecting her next bundle of joy and forget entirely about entering its predecessor's particulars in the Good Book.

Contributing numerous forks in Sarah's historical record are the array of surnames she acquired, including Bourjette, Bourdette, Bourget, Davis, Bowman, Borginnis, Boginnis, and perhaps, Foyle. Spelling errors could account for some, but she had a habit of taking a husband in a gather-ye-rosebuds-while-ye-may manner and often dispensed with bothersome formalities like marriage certificates and divorce decrees.

"The Great Western," written by acclaimed historian Nancy Hamilton for the Western Writers of America collection, *The Women Who Made the West*, puts Sarah's first documented appearance at Jefferson Barracks, Missouri, where in 1845, her husband enlisted in the Seventh Infantry.

In a manner of speaking, Sarah enlisted, as well, as a laundress. The position provided housing (in this case, a tent), full rations, fuel, medical care, and payment for laundering the soldiers' clothes at their expense. A proficient washerwomen could earn forty dollars a month, approximately three times an Army private's pay.

Regulations termed wives of officers and enlisted men as "camp followers," as they and other civilian employees followed the regiment from one bivouac or fort to the next. The term, also a euphemism for *prostitutes*, infuriated respectable military wives. Complain they surely did, but neither loudly nor often, for at any time, a commanding officer could banish a woman not working as a laundress.

The Amazonian Sarah was the burliest of the bunch by far, but denizens of Soapsuds Row who washboarded long-handles, shirts, and wool uniforms for a living were seldom shrinking violets. One was court-martialed for cursing an officer of the day. Another, charged with attempted murder, was marched off a post under fixed bayonets.

From Jefferson Barracks, the regiment to which Sarah and her husband were attached marched south to Corpus Christi Bay. Thus far, President Polk's attempts to buy or annex Mexico's claims to Texas and California had met with stubborn, diplomatic *gracias, pero ningunas gracias*. Negotiations continued, but the president wanted troops at ready in case force became the only option. And General Zachary Taylor was just the man Polk needed in Texas to get that job done.

Taylor's dragoons and camp followers arrived on the Nueces River at Corpus Christi in July 1845. By then, Sarah was also cooking for the regiment and nursing the injured and sick—her spouse, included.

A beachfront paradise it wasn't. Torrential downpours gave but temporary relief to windblown dust and sand, swarming insects, and the sun bearing down on countless tents rowed across the flats. For nine months, the regiment drilled and of-floaded supplies brought in by boat, their every move watched by hostile Mexicans on the river's opposite bank.

The conditions would be enough to make a saint cranky. Geography, topography, and weather were beyond Sarah's control, but when she got a bellyful of the evil eye in multiple, she told the camp commander, "If the general would give me a strong pair of tongs [slang for 'trousers'], I would wade the river and whip every scoundrel Mexican that dared show his face at the opposite side."

Realizing the Mexican government had no intention of ever relinquishing the disputed territory (though it had neither the means nor militia to defend it), in April 1846, Polk ordered General Taylor to march south toward the Rio Grande.

The Mexican cavalry was entrenched north of the river— itself a significant element of the boundary dispute, as it shifted course at Mother Nature's discretion. For either country to establish an immutable line of demarcation was virtually impossible.

General Taylor established a base at Port Isabel. A detachment, commanded by Major Jacob Brown, continued south to build an earthen fort across the river from Matamoros, Mexico. Sarah, astride a donkey pulling a cart full of cooking utensils, supplies, and luggage, was one of the few women who mobilized with Brown's fifty-man unit.

The Mexican cavalry regiment in Matamoros, led by General Arista, took a dim view of Major Brown's fife and drum– accompanied raising of the Stars and Stripes at dawn, then lowering at sunset. On April 24, Arista fired on the earthworks, christened Fort Taylor. Church bells in Matamoros pealed from the repercussion of a battery of eight-pounder cannon.

American troops returned fire. Enemy shells by the hundreds rent the air. Major Brown ordered the women to take cover behind the storage magazines and sew sandbags from the canvas tents.

Calmly insubordinate, Sarah Bowman proceeded to stoke the cook fire. In plain view of the enemy just across the river, the towering red-haired target ignored the screaming shells and bullets to bake bread and boil a cauldron of bean soup.

A "bullet through her bonnet and another through her bread tray" did not deter Sarah from delivering sustenance to the entrenched infantrymen or tending to the wounded.

The weeklong siege depleted ammunition and supplies, yet she continued to nurse the fallen, cook and serve the best meals she could muster. At night, she helped "her boys" write letters home.

She'd long been nicknamed the Great Western for the largest steamship of the day. After General Taylor's 2,300 incoming troops routed the enemy, she was hailed as the Heroine of Fort Brown—Fort Taylor having been renamed in honor of Major Brown, who perished from wounds sustained during the battle. (The site later became Brownsville, Texas.)

War was formally declared on May 13, 1846. Mexico didn't respond in kind for about six weeks, but by then, General Taylor's dragoons had taken Matamoros and were advancing up the Rio Grande.

Beginning with Matamoros, in each city captured and then occupied by American troops, Sarah established what one might call a full-service hotel. At her American House, a soldier could partake of room and board for six dollars a week, stable his horse for five, drink himself gotch-eyed, and be privately entertained by a female companion.

Those companions included the lusty, busty Sarah, who was now a widow—either in fact, or by merely declaring her soldier-husband dead to her. "You can imagine how tall she was," an apparently satisfied swain marveled. "She could stand flatfooted and drop these little sugarplums [nipples] right into my mouth, that way."

From Monterrey to Saltillo to Buena Vista, the American House(s)' proprietress camp-followed the army, serving up meals and medical care for the troops. Sarah's bravery under fire matched, if not exceeded, any soldier's. By several accounts, she was a one-woman ambulance, scooping up the wounded where they fell and carrying them to safety.

Zachary Taylor, a conservative in politics and attitude, didn't begrudge Sarah the profits reaped from her chain of hostels/saloons/bordellos. In his opinion, a happy soldier was a reliable soldier.

His approval of the troops' off-duty headquarters was not universal, due to the number of soldiers who returned to camp smiling but soused to the gills. Special Order 517 was issued in June 1847, stating that ". . . Mrs. Bourget [aka Sarah] having by permission of the General established a boardinghouse in the vicinity of the camp . . . be well understood that his permission is to be continued on condition that there shall not be a drop of liquor of any kind sold or kept at the establishment."

Prohibition may have negatively affected her income, but not her fervent patriotism or her respect for Zachary Taylor. The latter was evident (belatedly) to a deserter at Buena Vista, who beelined to her hotel in Saltillo, shouting that Taylor's defeat was imminent.

Sarah's roundhouse punch instantly reversed the messenger's trajectory and sent him flying boots over buttocks. "You damned son of a bitch, there ain't Mexicans enough in Mexico to whip old Taylor. You just spread that report and I'll beat you to death."

Legend had it that she'd already "... successfully defended herself with a saber while serving the gun [cannon]. She slew a Mexican who cut her across the cheek with his saber."

The Treaty of Guadalupe Hidalgo, ratified in July 1848, ended the war and, for a purchase price of fifteen million dollars, expanded the U.S territorial boundaries to include Texas, New Mexico, Arizona, Utah, Nevada, Wyoming, and part of Colorado.

Special Order 517's restrictions were voided, as well, but Sarah had been a camp follower too long to let her boys march on without her. She sought permission to join the expedition from Colonel Washington, who deferred to Major Rucker, who cited military regulations requiring that a laundress must also be a military wife.

"I'll marry the whole squadron and you thrown in but what I go along," she replied, and then mentioned, "Who wants a wife with fifteen thousand dollars and the biggest leg in Mexico?" Adding, "Come, my beauties, don't speak all at once—who is the lucky man?"

The upraised hand belonged to a soldier surnamed Davis, of Company E. Alas, the honeymoon ended abruptly, when Sarah spied a New Mexico trader whose height and muscular build surpassed her own. Those and other pertinent appraisals were most definitely in evidence, considering the man happened to be bathing at the time.

Trooper Davis was evicted from her tent posthaste, and Adonis moved in. Why the squadron's command didn't deem the substitution a violation of regulations is a mystery, but one can speculate that a six-feet-three-inch laundress who could stand in her new lover's shade encouraged a bit of rule-bending.

In early 1849, after recovering from an unnamed illness, Sarah arrived in El Paso, sans husband of any kind. A trader and merchant had already built a tavern, a warehouse, and corrals, anticipating the establishment of a military post.

Her timing for opening a new American House–El Paso couldn't have been better. The small, sleepy town was soon full to bursting with soldiers and hordes of gold-fevered prospectors racing west to California. Provisions were scarce and expensive, but the Great Western had plenty of experience at feeding the multitudes from a pint-sized pantry.

Not of the "settle down" persuasion, the Great Western moseyed on to Saltillo for a while, then opened the first restaurant in Arizona City (now Yuma). Around 1856, a patron of her saloon in Patagonia, Arizona, said, ". . . she packed two six-shooters and they all said she could use 'em," whereas a soldier stationed at Fort Yuma wrote,

> . . . She has been with the Army twenty years and was brought up here where she keeps the officers' mess. Among her other good qualities she is an admirable "pimp." She used to be a splendid looking woman and has done good service but is too old for that now.

Beauty being in the eye of the beholder, in 1860, Sarah acquired yet another husband, a German upholsterer named Albert J. Bowman, who was fifteen years her junior.

No angel was she, yet it's worth considering how her lifestyle would be judged in hindsight, had she been born male. Perhaps the army did just that, for the Heroine of Fort Brown received a full military funeral when she died—some say of a tarantula bite—on December 22, 1866.

She was the only woman buried in Fort Yuma's cemetery. Later, all the graves were disinterred for reburial at the Presidio National Cemetery, including Sarah Bowman's.

Which was only fitting, as where else would General Zachary Taylor's bravest camp follower rather spend eternity than with "her boys."

5

MARGARET "MOLLY" BROWN

"Women first" is a principle as deep-rooted in man's being as the sea.
It is world-old and irrevocable, but to me it is all wrong.
Women demand equal rights on land—why not at sea?

J ust about anyone who recognizes the name Molly Brown connects it to the *Titanic* disaster and her portrayal on screen and on stage in *The Unsinkable Molly Brown.*

Which is a damned shame, since the Hollywood and Broadway versions fictionalized fiction, starting with the title character's name. Margaret Tobin Brown never ever went by Molly. The nickname was just easier for lyricists to put to music.

The true story of Margaret's life is as fascinating and certainly more admirable than the Annie Oakley–meets–Calamity Jane bushwah manufactured by newspaperman Gene Fowler and tourist-brochure-writer Caroline Bancroft, and perpetuated by the play, several movies (including James Cameron's *Titanic*), a radio show, and numerous books and articles.

Another, broader misconception affected Margaret throughout her life: that the Irish were a class by themselves—an irrefutably and unredeemable *low* class of the "can't make a silk purse from a sow's ear" persuasion.

Part of the prejudice stemmed from religious intolerance for "papists," as those of the Catholic faith were then termed. The Irish who emigrated to escape the potato famine were also largely illiterate. Not due to innate stupidity, as their detractors chose to believe, but because England had banned education of any kind to subjugate and isolate the Irish and thus minimize revolts against oppressive British rule.

Margaret's parents, John and Johanna Tobin, were fresh-off-the-boat Irish and proud of it. When they met in Hannibal, Missouri, both were widowed single parents. John's daughter, Caroline, was a year older than Johanna's daughter, Mary Ann. Son Daniel was born in 1863, then Margaret, on July 18, 1867. Another son, William, and daughter, Helen, expanded the Tobin brood to an even half-dozen.

After the Civil War, Hannibal thrived as a river- and railroad town. The growing Irish workforce mostly stayed to its side of the tracks, with the church the hub of social activities.

Though John Tobin's job at the Hannibal Gas Works kept the family fed and clothed, luxuries were few, and for John, leisure time was nonexistent. Margaret later said her father's life was "bounded by working and sleeping."

A four-room house on Denkler Alley gave scant elbow room for a family of eight, but Margaret often reflected fondly on her childhood. The Mississippi was a rock-throw from the back door. A thick copse of trees strung with rope swings galore was a favorite playground—and the probable genesis of

Gene Fowler's fable regarding Mark Twain fishing nearby when a cyclone dropped a bewildered but uninjured Margaret Tobin.

Hannibal's other claim to fame allegedly dubbed the tomboy who whistled like a calliope and swam like a porpoise, "a female Huckleberry Finn," adding that the child wasn't even aware she was a girl.

Just because Samuel Clemens, later known as Mark Twain, left town fourteen years before Margaret Tobin drew first breath didn't keep the yarn Fowler spun in the 1930s from gaining acceptance and endless repetition as fact.

Hannibal established a (segregated) public school system in 1859, and several private schools were available, but Margaret and her siblings learned their three R's from their aunt Mary O'Leary and later, her daughter.

By custom born of necessity and her status as working-class Irish, thirteen-year-old Margaret hired on at D.J. Garth & Bro. Tobacco Company's factory. Separating tobacco leaves from their stems was as physically demanding and dead-end a job as they come. Long hours in a hot, muggy factory earned a pittance compared with what the exclusively male cigar-rollers were paid. Her alternatives—working as a maid or a store clerk—weren't much easier and paid less.

In 1883, Margaret's brother Daniel, her half sister Mary Ann and her husband, Jack Landrigan, ventured west to Leadville, then the fastest-growing town in the United States. Two years later, Daniel wired train fare to Margaret, who leapt at the chance to keep house for him.

As usual, the got-rich-quick stories vastly outnumbered prospectors who'd prized a fortune from the mines, but she "longed to be rich enough to give [her father] a home so he would not have to work."

The cost of living in any western boomtown was far higher than anywhere else, simply because most sprang up overnight in the middle of nowhere. While Denver City had erupted on Colorado's flat, low-lying Eastern plains, Leadville's elevation exceeded ten thousand feet and lay like a crown jewel in the cleave between the Sawatch Range to the west and the Mosquito Range to the east.

By the time Margaret arrived, a railroad line connected the "top of Colorado" town to Denver City and beyond, except a region where better than twenty feet of snow falls per year isn't what one would call readily accessible.

To supplement Daniel's earnings at a mine, Margaret found work as a sewer in the carpet and drapery department at the Daniels, Fisher and Smith dry goods store. Back in Hannibal, they'd be in tall cotton on their combined wages. In a town where flour sold for $3.50 a sack, they barely scraped by.

"It is a truth universally acknowledged, that a single man in possession of a good fortune, must be in want of a wife," said Jane Austen. In the case of James Joseph Brown, so does a fortune-hoper infatuated with a red-haired seamstress.

Somewhat to her chagrin, Margaret was equally attracted to the tall, handsome, charming Irishman who was employed as a shift manager for a mining conglomerate. His was a reasonably well-paying job, but not nearly enough to support a wife and her dream of financing John Tobin's retirement from the Gas Works before he worked himself into an early grave.

"I wanted a rich man," she later said, "but I loved Jim Brown."

After their church wedding on September 1, 1886, the couple settled in Jim's two-room cabin in Stumpftown, which one old-timer said "got its personality from the pool hall." Its ambience, no doubt, came from the smoky, sooty haze of scores of coal- and woodburning stoves and the outhouses teetering behind every cabin.

A community well supplied all the water the new Mrs. Brown needed for drinking, cooking, bathing, cleaning, and laundering Jim's grimy clothes—once she lugged it by the bucketful back up to the cabin. Winter's heavy snowfall wasn't entirely a bane, as melting it on the stove surely saved countless trips to the well.

Privation and primiparahood sent Margaret home to Hannibal for the birth of her son, Lawrence Palmer Brown, on August 30, 1887. She and Jim then moved back to Leadville, and Margaret hired a tutor to further her interests in literature and music.

The next few years were among the happiest of her life. Her brother Daniel wed his longtime sweetheart, Mary Brophy Grace. With their four oldest children and families now living in Leadville, John and Johanna Tobin packed up teenagers Will and Helen and migrated west. Jim Brown, now superintendent of the Maid and Henriette Mining Company, got his sixty-year-old father-in-law a job as a watchman.

On July 1, 1889, Margaret gave birth to Catherine Ellen, whom they called Helen. Two small children and a husband fast becoming a "top flight mining man" didn't interfere with her involvement in charity work. Wives of prosperous men were expected to donate hours and energy to civic fund-raising activities and hospital work, but Margaret didn't stop at that.

Organizing soup kitchens for destitute miners and their families didn't endear her to their employers (her own husband included). Many of the needy were immigrants. Some spoke little or no English. All had come to Leadville to make better lives for themselves. Margaret's conscience simply couldn't abide the profits of their labor putting food on her table while they went hungry.

The doyennes of Leadville couldn't fault her for feeding the poor, so they launched a personal, behind-the-hand whisper campaign. Mrs. Brown was getting a mite big for her shanty Irish britches—too quick to speak her mind about women's suffrage and miners' rights. And dear heavens, the woman "painted her face," and at the time no proper lady indulged in cosmetic artifice.

Leadville's political and economic playing field leveled abruptly in October 1893 when Congress repealed the Sherman Silver Purchase Act. Instead of bimetalism (gold *and* silver coins) the repeal reinstituted the gold standard.

The price of silver plummeted. By the following summer, 90 percent of what remained of Leadville's mine workers were unemployed.

It's no exaggeration to say the Little Jonny silver mine, part of the Ibex Mining Company's holdings of which Jim Brown was a shareholder, saved Leadville's descent to a ghost town. When Ibex's owners announced intentions to make a gold mine out of the Little Jonny, the *Leadville Herald Democrat* warned, "there were probably 1,000 men each of whom had 25,000 reasons why gold should not be found there."

Shortly thereafter, the same newspaper boasted, "the little Jonnie[sic] is shipping 135 tons of good ore per day."

Jim and Margaret Brown had struck it rich. His overnight success had taken only twenty years of backbreaking work.

In time, newfound wealth bought a custom-built, foursquare Victorian mansion on four hundred acres outside Denver, closetsful of Parisian gowns for Margaret, the couple's inclusion in the Denver Social Register . . . and frequent, not-so-subtle allusions on the wind and in the newspapers regarding Jim Brown's wandering eye.

Rumors of his adulterous liaisons had blistered Margaret's ears in Leadville, but now Lawrence and Helen were old enough to be hurt and embarrassed by the gossipmongering. So were Daniel Tobin's three children, whom Margaret had taken under her wing following the death of their mother. Divorce wasn't in a devout Catholic's vocabulary. Margaret proceeded to grin, bear it, and throw herself into a raft of social, charitable, and political activities.

As alleged, the Browns were not among the Sacred Thirty-six, the name derived from self-appointed icon Louise Crawford Hill's snipe that only thirty-six Denverites met her criteria for social standing. It was the same old cavil, different town: the Browns were too Irish, too Catholic, too nouveau riche. Margaret's politics were too liberal, and she too liberally and loudly expressed them.

The slight wasn't lost on Margaret, but it merely nicked her pride, rather than gouged it. According to Kristen Iversen's biography, "From 1894 to the early 20s, the Browns took up more space in Denver's society pages than nearly any other Denver family . . . ," and despite demeaning portrayals of Margaret/Molly to the contrary, ". . . [the Browns] were not ostracized by Denver society—they *were* Denver society."

Margaret *was* devastated by the fourth estate's very public heyday with the fifty-thousand-dollar alienation-of-affection suit filed against Jim Brown by his lover's cuckholded husband. The suit was eventually settled out of court, but Margaret began spending almost as much time away from Denver as in it.

Between numerous European sojourns, her estimable accomplishments included charter membership in the Denver Woman's Club, membership in the Denver Women's Press Club, and fund-raising events to underwrite an expansion to St. Joseph's Hospital.

Partnered with Judge Ben Lindsey, Margaret hounded officials for a separate juvenile justice system. Incarcerating hardened criminals with youthful offenders was "a school for crime—deliberately teaching them to be horse thieves and safecrackers."

Perhaps Margaret's most controversial endeavor was managing the Carnival of Nations to fund completion of Cathedral Parish (later called Denver's most beautiful church). Inspired by the World's Fair, the Carnival was an international living history showcase that, to the consternation of many Denverites, included a Chinese exposition and a re-created Indian village.

Asian immigrants had always been and still were considered an anathema. The "only good Indian, is a dead Indian" attitude prevailed less than forty years removed from the last battle between the U.S. Army and Plains Indians of Colorado.

The efforts of a supposed pillar of the community threatened to shut down the Carnival weeks sooner than scheduled. Margaret's compromise, to donate some proceeds to a Juvenile Improvement Association project, met with a flat refusal, purely for political reasons. Although the Carnival closed early, Margaret then "claim-jumped" a defunct mine in Cripple Creek, reopened it, and declared all profits would be donated to the juvenile court system.

By the twentieth century's first decade, the woman later caricatured as a vulgar, blowsy, uneducated forerunner to Lucy Ricardo was fluent in five languages and had studied literature and language at the Carnegie Technical Schools, later renamed The Carnegie Institute.

As for Margaret's personal life, if ever the term *irreconcilable differences* applied to a couple, it did Jim and Margaret Brown. For years, he'd resented his wife's globe-trotting, political ambitions and devotion to social reform—that is, a "good wife" doesn't run for Congress. She keeps the home fires burning and warms her beloved's slippers by them.

By nature, Margaret wasn't the type to sit around darning socks for a man who seldom slept in his own bed and was seldom alone in strange ones.

A psychology degree isn't required to deduce that the marriage of a chauvinist libertine to a strong-willed monogamous feminist must have more than two children and memories of good times to survive.

On January 24, 1910, a newspaper reporter thought Jim and Margaret were spending the holidays on opposite coasts. Knowing their names boosted circulation, he announced the couple's divorce had been finalized.

"In the face of our Catholic religion," Margaret responded, "we could not think of divorce," but did subsequently admit a formal separation agreement was signed several months prior.

Outside the realms of Colorado and Newport, Rhode Island

(her summer home for several years), the rest of Margaret To-bin Brown's life might have passed in peaceful obscurity—had she not received word while in England that Lawrence's son—her first grandchild—had fallen ill.

The H.M.S. *Titanic*'s maiden voyage was the fastest means available to return to the United States. If not for her daughter's last-minute change of plans, Helen would also have been aboard when a glacier eviscerated the unsinkable luxury liner's hull.

Aside from Margaret passengering Lifeboat No. 6, virtually every "fact" attributed to her six-hour ordeal at sea was fictionalized, if not outright prevarication. Realizing the ship was sinking, she purposely donned a velvet two-piece suit, a sable stole, and seven pairs of wool stockings for warmth. She gave extra wool stockings to other hypothermic passengers, but the stories of her extensive wardrobe being distributed widely are pure invention.

Nor did she belt out, "I'm unsinkable," or "Row, you sons-a-bitches!" or lead a rousing songfest. Voices raised in song echoed from several lifeboats that night . . . to muffle the pitiful cries and moans of the dying adrift in life preservers, or clinging to pieces of flotsam. Later, the survivors sang to mask the unrelieved silence.

Margaret did not wrest command of the lifeboat at pistol-point from Quartermaster Hichens. Lucky for him, she *wasn't* armed, for as Iverson's biography relates, Margaret wrote of him in an article published in newspapers nationwide,

We had in our boat one creature—I will not call him a man,
for we had no way of knowing it except by his clothes, so

craven was he. This creature kept crying out that all was lost, that we might as well give up . . . [As soon as] we pulled into the boat a poor, half-frozen stoker, we had evidence of manhood. This almost naked man I wrapped in my sable stole, and when the craven creature, the quartermaster, talked impudently to me, and when, tired of his complaints, I threatened to have him thrown overboard, the stoker rebuked him.

The doctor on board the rescue ship, the *Carpathia*, also received the sharp side of Margaret's tongue when he discouraged her and other first-class passengers from aiding and comforting second- and steerage-class survivors. Not that all the wealthy aboard the rescue ship were generous with their compassion or their cash. At Margaret's request for pledges to provide shelter for the destitute in New York, several society matrons said they'd be accommodated at the Waldorf, and the less fortunate were none of their concern.

After the *Carpathia* docked in New York, Margaret stayed aboard until the following day to act as a translator and ensure penniless immigrants weren't deported posthaste.

A headline in the April 12, 1912, edition of the *Denver Post* read: H.R. ROOD AND MRS. BROWN CERTAINLY SAILED ON TITANIC and noted, oddly, in the text, "The Denver society woman is the most heavily insured woman in Colorado, carrying insurance amounting to $135,000 on her life." The presumed beneficiary, Jim Brown, remarked, "She's too mean to sink"—which, ironically, may have credenced the "Unsinkable" label.

The most degrading aspect of the burlesque-style fabrications attached to Margaret Brown's survival is that, like the other fortunate few hundred, memories of the tragedy haunted her for the rest of her life. To trivialize the disaster with scenes such as "Molly," seated in the lifeboat watching the bisected liner's final plunge and joking, "Now there's something you don't see every day!" dishonors the more than 1,500 who perished.

When Margaret Tobin Brown died of a brain tumor on October 13, 1932, the *Rocky Mountain News* averred that as a young, pigtailed tomboy, she'd spent long afternoons on the banks of the Mississippi playing with Mark Twain.

A *Denver Post* reporter portrayed her truthfully and respectfully: "Not being a man, she determined to be a successful woman, to see this world, to meet its best and be one of them."

In Margaret's own words, "Money can't make man or woman. . . . It isn't who you are, or what you have, but what you are that counts."

(Alaska Historical Society)

6

NELLIE CASHMAN

You never quite know what's going to happen next,
or when your time will come to cash in your checks.
It all adds interest and variety to life.

Few women in the nineteenth century, or certainly the
twentieth, lived a more interesting and varied life than
Miss Nellie Cashman.

Born in Queenstown, County Cork, Ireland, in about 1850,
Nellie emigrated to Boston in the early 1860s with her older
sister Frances and their widowed mother. Since the Civil War
had decreased the available manpower, women were being
hired to fill what had been traditionally male occupations.

According to Frank Cullen Brophy's article, "God And Nellie," her first job in that city afforded her an opportunity to meet
a man who would later become President of the United States.

"I remember when I met General Ulysses S. Grant," Nellie
said.

I was a bellhop in Boston at the time. He was easy to talk to, like everyone I ever knew, and when I told him I wanted to do things, because I had to if I wanted to live, he said, "Why don't you go West, young woman? The West needs people like you."

Well, we had gone west when we left Ireland, and I certainly didn't expect to spend the rest of my life being a bellhop or an Irish servant girl in Boston.

The two elder Cashmans must have agreed with Nellie's and General Grant's idea of manifest destiny. That, or Nellie's stubbornness won the debate. By 1869, the trio was en route to San Francisco on the newly completed transcontinental railroad.

A special immigrant rate of forty dollars entitled them to space on a springless railroad car fitted with backless board seats. Those "bargain fare" cars were routinely shunted onto sidings to allow express trains the right-of-way. The two-thousand-mile journey, accomplished at an average speed of eighteen- to twenty-two hot, dusty miles per hour, must have given passengers a graphic example of "hell on wheels."

Upon their arrival, Frances soon wed fellow Irishman Thomas Cunningham and settled in the City by the Bay to start a family.

Nellie's petite and comely figure, shining black eyes and hair, fair complexion, and beguiling brogue must have attracted a host of suitors, but romance didn't stand a chance against her wanderlust.

Instead, she set two goals for herself: to make a lot of money, and to help anyone who needed it. At both she became eminently successful.

Her skill with a spatula got her hired as a cook in several western mining camps. Precisely when she traded a frying pan for a gold pan is unknown, but in 1877, Nellie was prospecting in the Cassiar Mountain District of British Columbia. Dressed in a mackinaw, men's trousers, boots, and a fur hat, she was the first white woman to behold the beauty and treachery of that snow-covered wilderness.

"I went north to Cassiar with a party of 200 miners from Nevada," she said later during a newspaper interview.

We penetrated a practically unknown country. When the party settled down in what was then a very rich region, I alternately mined and kept a boarding house for miners.

In the fall of the year I came out to civilization, that is to Victoria [B.C.], but learning that a large number of our party was sick with the scurvy, I hastened back after securing six men to accompany me.

It took 77 days to reach camp as the winter was very severe. At [Fort] Wrangel the United States custom officers tried to dissuade me from taking what they termed "my mad trip," and in fact, when we had been several days up the river on our journey, they sent up a number of men to induce me to turn back.

Actually, an Indian had reported a white woman's death to Fort Wrangel's commander. The officer knew Nellie was the only white woman within hundreds of miles and dispatched soldiers to find her body. Find her they did—relaxing beside a roaring campfire, contentedly sipping a cup of tea.

"We pushed on, however, in the coldest kind of weather

with hardly any trail to follow and after sleeping 66 days in the snow, reached the camp in time to be of service to the men, some of whom were half-dead for want of proper supplies."

After that adventure's happy ending, Nellie reentered the Lower 48 a wealthier woman for having gained the admiration and respect of her prospecting peers, and extensive, hands-on mining experience. But with the boom all but busted in Nevada, Nellie meandered south to investigate rumors of strikes in California's arid hinterlands.

As she later told a reporter for the *Arizona Star*, Nellie and the other stagecoach passengers were jostling along a rough-cut track across the barrens when the driver suddenly reined his team to a halt. " 'What dump is this?' I called, 'The City of Angels?' There was nothing, absolutely nothing, but dogs in sight. It was the first time I knew that dogs had souls. . . . "

I came very near being a pioneer of California, but those dogs and Los Angeles cured me. So we bumped along over trails into Yuma. Such a place—mosquitoes by the billions everywhere. When we sat down to supper, I asked the driver if he hadn't seasoned the beans rather heavily with pepper.

He looked up and laughed, "Mosquitoes it is, my friend," he said. But we ate the beans just the same. Had to. There was nothing else cooked.

Nellie disembarked in Tucson, Arizona Territory, but quickly decided the sleepy, Mexican pueblo would likely remain that way even after the Southern Pacific Railroad began servicing it.

Eighty-miles-distant Tombstone, located in an incredibly

rich silver-bearing area, had already gained a "lively" reputation. Nellie wasted precious little time transferring her residency to the town Ed Schieffelin's Lucky Cuss Mine had founded.

The Nevada Boot & Shoe Store, a general mercantile at Allen and Fifth, was her first enterprise, followed by the acquisition of the Arcade, a restaurant specializing in steaks and chops. Soon after the eatery opened, however, Cashman sold the Arcade—as it happened, a most fortuitously timed divestiture. Within weeks, the Arcade's cigar-puffing bartender was hefting a barrel of bad whiskey onto the porch when embers from his stogie fell inside. The alcohol exploded, setting off a fiery chain reaction that left the Arcade and much of Tombstone's business district naught but a smoldering memory.

In partnership with cattle rancher Joseph Pascholy, Nellie established and managed another restaurant, the Russ House, at the corner of Fifth and Tough Nut streets.

Because Tombstone's whiskey-addled miners were known to swipe cats to ensure a rodent-free night's sleep, Nellie's declaration that "There are no cockroaches in my kitchen and the flour is clean," was especially meaningful. Scrupulous sanitation, plus a menu featuring "the best food this side of the Pecos," allowed her to charge double the going rate of twenty-five cents per meal.

And what a meal that paltry four bits would buy: a choice of two soups, two fish dishes, three kinds of boiled meat, entrées ranging from "Breast of lamb, breaded a la Mayonnaise" to "Calf Head in Tortue," roasted beef (two cuts), pork, or chicken, leg of mutton, stuffed lamb, or dressed veal, five vegetables, two pastries, two puddings, grapes and walnuts, lobster, tomato, beet, or horseradish salad, and assorted relishes.

No wonder more than four hundred people elbowed into the Russ House's dining room on opening day. But Cashman's already well-known reputation for treating down-on-their-luck prospectors to free meals presumes the crowd probably included a number of nonpaying customers.

Nellie also became a sort of one-woman chamber of commerce and Salvation Army commandant combined. Shoot-'em-up reputation or no, Tombstone and its citizenry were soon wrapped around her little finger.

Her fund-raising abilities were later recounted by ardent admirer and *Tombstone Epitaph* founder-editor John Clum: "If she asked for a contribution—we contributed. If she had tickets to sell—we bought tickets. If she needed actors for a play—we volunteered to act. And although Nellie's pleas were frequent, none ever refused her."

The moneys she raised helped construct one of the city's first schools and the Sacred Heart of Jesus Catholic Church. The latter project stemmed from Nellie's concern that although the Methodists, Presbyterians, and Episcopalians had flourishing houses of worship, the Catholics had none at all. The bishop in charge of the diocese agreed that a church was needed and made a bargain with her: If Nellie provided the building, he'd come up with a priest.

She was certainly assigned the more difficult task, but had no qualms about canvasing the entire town for contributions, including the "wrong" side of Allen Street, which was strewn with saloons, gambling houses, and the red-light district.

Nellie evidently agreed with Episcopalian rector Reverend Endicott Peabody's philosophy that "The Lord's pot must be kept boiling even if it takes the Devil's kindling wood."

After raising seven hundred dollars by personal subscription, Nellie organized additional fund-raisers, including Tombstone's first amateur theater production (a musical comedy titled *The Irish Diamond*) and a grand ball.

The proceeds fulfilled her end of the bargain. True to his word, no sooner than the new church was finished, the bishop assigned Father Gallagher to serve as its priest.

For all her public philanthropy, in late 1880, Nellie's energies turned toward helping her destitute sister. Frances's husband had died of tuberculosis, leaving her with five small children and no means of support.

Nellie brought her grief-stricken sister, by now also in ill health, and the children to Tombstone. The humble adobe cottage they lived in behind the Russ House must have been packed chock-a-block with the Cunningham clan and their possessions, but Nellie never complained about the additional work or responsibilities she'd taken on.

Within three years, Frances succumbed to tuberculosis, leaving "Aunt Nell" to raise and educate her three nieces and two nephews, ranging in age from four to twelve years old.

Her involvement with a different quintet raised hackles in several quarters. In the nearby town of Bisbee, on the evening of December 8, 1883, Daniel Dowd, Omer W. Sample, James Howard, William Delaney, and Daniel Kelly robbed Goldwater & Castenada's Store. The thieves' indiscriminate gunfire amidst a crowd of innocent Christmas shoppers left one woman and two men dead, and another man slowly bleeding to death in the dusty street.

The perpetrators of the "Bisbee Massacre" were soon arrested, tried, convicted, and sentenced to hang. Nellie had no doubts about their guilt, but was appalled to learn a grandstand was being built and tickets sold for five hundred spectators to witness the grisly execution. Rumor also had it that the murderers' bodies would be disinterred from their Boot Hill graves and sold as medical cadavers.

Nellie believed that justice would not be served by such un-Christian, inhumane treatment. Her deep and abiding faith probably caused her to also despair for the crowd's immortal souls if the circuslike event proceeded as planned.

At about two, scant hours before the condemned men were due to meet their Maker, Nellie and a band of miners she'd recruited to help advanced on the scaffold. Wielding crowbars, sledgehammers, picks, axes, and doublejacks, the wrecking crew quickly reduced the grandstand to kindling.

"When the mob showed up for the hanging, next morning," Nellie was quoted as saying, "they found the bleachers and benches blown to smithereens. Nobody cashed in on that hanging, and when they called the show off, I think most of them were secretly glad we had stopped them."

Tombstone's mine shafts soon started to flood. Profits dwindled and several mine owners decreased their workers' daily wages from four dollars to three. Outraged by the pay cut, union employees of the Grand Central Mine, one of the largest, went out on strike.

Nellie likely supported the miners' grievances, but her sympathies didn't extend to ignoring a plot to kidnap and lynch E. B. Gage, the Grand Central's manager.

Calmly buggying out to the home of the necktie party's guest of honor, Nellie alerted Gage to the danger and drove him back through town at a pace conducive to lovers on a Sunday afternoon ride. Once they'd passed Tombstone's outskirts, Nellie yee-hawed the team pell-mell toward the railroad station at Benson, where Gage boarded a train for Tucson—and safety.

While she saved Gage from a premature funeral, not even the indomitable Miss Cashman could alter Tombstone's fate. People were packing up and moving on in droves, just as they'd arrived a few years earlier. When the tax base could no longer support the school system, Nellie locked the Russ House's door for the last time.

Nieces and nephews in tow, she prospected in Montana and Wyoming, hoping for a gold strike big enough to support her foster family. No bonanzas came her way, but enough ore kept bodies and souls together. Except frontier mining camps were hardly a fit place to raise children, and few had schools.

Rather than a catch-as-catch-can education, Nellie enrolled the Cunningham children in Catholic boarding schools in California. From there, she drifted to Kingston, New Mexico, then the Harquahala, Mina Prietas, and the Preston fields in Arizona Territory. Such geographic hopscotching was likely indicative of minimal mining success.

The next published account of Nellie's travels appeared in late November 1889 in Tucson's *Arizona Star*: "Miss Nellie Cashman is visiting with Mrs. E.J. Smith of this city. Miss Cashman has just returned from a trip to Africa and is here in search of a group to accompany her to that country to explore a hitherto unheard of diamond region."

Whether Nellie ever went to Africa—which historical record doesn't support, much less confirm—she certainly never returned there. By the fall of 1897, news of an enormous strike in the Canadian Yukon set her course for the next quarter century.

From her dockside arrival at Skagway, Alaska, she undertook a rugged, six-hundred-mile trek by dogsled and on foot, lugging nine hundred pounds of supplies. The grueling Chilkoot Pass defeated thousands of burly, back-strong men, but not a nigh fifty-year-old (or older) veteran prospector renowned as America's only female mining expert.

She staked her claims, actively prospected, and operated several small businesses in Dawson. One room in her mercantile was nicknamed The Prospector's Haven of Rest because miners were welcome to partake of free coffee, tobacco, and cigars while reading or writing letters home.

In return, the grubstakers honored Nellie with the sobriquet "the Miner's Angel" and treated her with the utmost respect and admiration. It was said that her entrance to any establishment in town was the signal for every man in the room to stand.

Despite her five decades of predominantly male companionship, when asked why she'd never married, Nellie laughed and said, "Marriage? I haven't had time for marriage. Men are a nuisance anyhow, aren't they?"

However, Victorian conventions regarding ladylike conduct were as inflexible as whaleboned corsets. A virtuous, enterprising pioneer like Nellie Cashman presented an anomaly—an exception to the "rules."

In that era, unmarried women who routinely cohabitated with men were usually labeled strumpets or Jezebels. Ironically, according to an anecdote in Frances H. Backhouse's article, "Women of the Klondike," Nellie was once turned away from a trail camp after supper because the men "feared for her reputation—or theirs—if she was allowed to remain in camp after dark."

Although her atypical lifestyle and prospecting pursuits made her a trailblazer in every sense of the word, not a whisper of scandal ever tarnished Nellie's name or her sterling reputation.

Once, she was bluntly asked if she had ever "feared for her virtue."

"Bless your soul, no!" she answered.

I never had a word said to me that was out of the way. The "boys" would see to it that anyone who ever offered to insult me could never be able to repeat the offense.

The farther you go away from civilization, the bigger-hearted and more courteous you find the men. Every man I met up north was my protector and any man I ever met, if he needed my help, got it, whether it was a hot meal, nursing, mothering, or whatever else he needed. After all, we pass this way only once, and it's up to us to help our fellows when they need our help.

That selfless attitude, as well as a burning desire to strike it rich prospecting, were deeply ingrained long before Nellie washed an ounce of precious, dull-yellow flakes from a streambed's sandy residue.

She prized over one hundred thousand dollars in gold from the ground around Dawson, later admitting she "spent every red cent of it buying other claims and prospecting the country."

By then it was apparent that finding gold was not enough; she dreamed of nothing less than the Mother Lode:

I've suffered trials and hardships in the frozen plains of Alaska and on the deserts of Arizona. I've been alone all my life but I have been happy and healthy. That's why all are fooled about my age. And that is why I'm not afraid like most women to tell you that I'm 67 and that I'm mighty apt to make a million or two before I leave this romantic business of mining.

Believing that elusive million might lie farther north, Nellie moved to a camp in the midst of the Arctic Circle. Her incredibly isolated, nearly top-of-the-world new home was appropriately named Coldfoot. It was so remote that on the first leg of her 1923 trip to the States to visit relatives, Nellie mushed a sled along icy trails for seventeen days just to leave the frigid wilderness *surrounding* Coldfoot. And when she undertook the 750-mile trek, alone but for her dog team, the Miner's Angel was at least seventy years old.

Despite Nellie's never-say-die grit and incredible hardiness, time had taken its inevitable toll. Late in 1924, she contracted double pneumonia and was transported by boat to a hospital in Fairbanks. Although visibly weakened and frail, she was dismissed a few weeks later.

Convinced that Coldfoot would yield the bonanza she'd spent most of her life trying to find, she went to Victoria, British Columbia, to seek investors willing to finance the sinking of a new shaft. By the time she arrived, her iron constitution was failing.

Ever the strong-willed Irish lass, upon her admission to Victoria's St. Joseph's Hospital, she refused the use of a wheelchair and walked to her room. Perhaps she felt she deserved a more dignified entrance. After all, a half-century before, her and other Cassiar miners' contributions had helped *build* that facility.

"Sometimes I can hardly wait until I can get together Up There with all them fellers I used to know," she once remarked. "Say, won't we do some mining, though? And yarns! Why, I bet there's never been yarns like the ones we'll spin when I get there."

If such an eternal reunion is possible, it commenced for Nellie Cashman on January 4, 1925. According to her wishes, she was interred beside the Sisters of St. Ann's plot, on a bluff overlooking the Pacific, in Victoria's Ross Bay Cemetery.

Newspapers throughout North America eulogized her—a few bordered her obituary in black; a respectful gesture usually reserved for public officials and high-ranking dignitaries.

The *Arizona Star* declared that

> ... she lived on through the years of hardships that would have broken many men, to the ripe age of nearly eighty, though reports given out were that she was seventy. Pioneers, however, count differently and declare their addition good.
>
> The "old sourdough" has passed on, leaving many records behind—pioneer of Arizona, the first woman prospector in Alaska, the world's champion musher—but better by far than all of these is the fact that she lived—lived and enjoyed adventures that it is not given most the courage to taste.

Only a carved curbstone inscribed NELLIE CASHMAN; JANUARY 4, 1925; 80 [SIC] YEARS; BORN IN IRELAND marks her grave. It is not a proper epitaph for one who gave so much and expected so little. She wasn't a saint and surely had her faults, including a bit o' the blarney when reporters were in the vicinity. Yet perhaps one day a monument will be erected to honor the bonny Irish immigrant whose pioneering spirit, like her generosity and courage, seemed inexhaustible.

And on it, a plaque with the eloquently simple words her friend and fellow Tombstonian Fred Dodge used to describe her: "A truly remarkable and admirable woman."

In 1993, the United States Postal Service issued a commemorative series of stamps, postcards, envelopes, and a book titled "Legends of the West." Nellie Cashman was one of twenty depictions included in the collection.

(Library of Congress, LC–USZ62-50017)

7

LAURA FAIR

He would shoot over the head of my bed, sir, with a pistol.
Then he would go out and shoot the poultry in the yard,
fifty at a time, one after another.

It could and has been said that the fetching Miss Fair gave romance her best shot. Unfortunately, it ventilated her intended target in a most fatal manner.

Born a Southern belle in 1837, precious little of her background is known, apart from a string of ill-fated marches down the aisle. What's curious is whether she earned her historic portrayal as loose (let alone lethal), or if that was the product of nineteenth-century-style spin.

Laura first married at the age of sixteen, but was widowed within a year. The phrase *mysterious circumstances* is invariably applied to the wedding's date, locale, and identity of the groom, as well as to his cause of death.

Husband number two didn't fare much better, but he did

survive his holy wedlock with Laura. He was often drunk, and would dispatch innocent household furnishings and poultry, which gained Laura a divorce—presumably before he turned temperate and his aim improved.

In the early 1860s, Laura owned a boardinghouse in Virginia City, Nevada. Either before or during her stint as a landlady, she trod a San Francisco stage in the role of Lady Teazle in a production of *School for Scandal*.

While the play's title would later seem both an irony and an augury, one newspaper reviewer was effusive in his praise for Miss Fair's acting debut, saying she "had put to the blush many of the professionals [in the cast]."

Talented a thespian as she may have been, a self-inflicted version of the proverbial .22-caliber divorce left Laura a widow for a second time. As the story goes, her third husband didn't take it in stride when she announced her affections had alienated to another.

Not one to let no luck at love deter her, while in Virginia City, Laura made the acquaintance of Alexander Parker Crittendon, a San Francisco attorney. For six months, Crittendon wooed Miss Fair's heart, then won it with a proposal of marriage.

Either pillow-talk discussions of when and where the nuptials should be performed, or a continuing lack of specificity on Crittendon's part led to the revelation that a divorce from the current Mrs. Crittendon was in order, before Laura started shopping for her trousseau.

According to some sources, Crittendon was hoping for a European-style arrangement—a home complete with a wife and children, and a mistress on the side. All very continental and civilized.

Not, however, what Laura had in mind. Considerably well-practiced at being a legal wife, rather than tell her lover to go fly a kite in a thunderstorm, she must have issued the same ultimatum women have since time immemorial: Get a divorce, or get out of my life.

Crittendon's response must have been the equally hoary, "I promise, I will, darling, just give me a little time," for Laura waited and waited and waited for him to make an honest woman of her.

Although originally the nickname for a prolonged, scabies-type skin irritation, the phrase *seven-year itch* became synonymous with marital boredom, particularly in the bedroom. In Laura Fair's case, seven years of Crittendon's excuses had her trigger-finger itching for revenge.

Knowing her lover was to meet his family at the Oakland ferry, Laura arrived just in time to see Crittendon embrace his wife. Laura leveled the pistol her lover had allegedly encouraged her to carry, took aim at his duplicitous heart, shouted, "You have ruined me!" and fired.

Laura was arrested in the ferry's saloon, where she confessed to the crime. Crittendon lingered for a day or so, but in that era, few recovered from a point-blank gunshot wound to the chest.

Lisle Lester, a freelance writer and correspondent for several Bay Area newspapers, took keen interest in the case. So did the president and several members of a California state women's suffrage organization. Ms. Lester deemed herself a politically objective journalist, yet automatically sided with the defendant.

"Not so much because of the evidence, as because the murderer was a woman," Fay Campbell Kaynor states in Lisle's biography, *Lapdogs and Bloomer Girls*. ". . . males [such as Crittendon] who were enjoying the double standard responsible for this woman's distress were to be her jury, judge, and appointed hangman."

Miss Lisle's appraisal had merit. The Sixth Amendment guarantee of a jury, as Blackstone defined, "of twelve of his equals and neighbors indifferently chosen and superior to all suspicion" could be construed as thirteen-against-one in instances where a defendant was female, and the individual she was accused of killing and the dozen deciding her fate were all male.

Bias of another stripe was levied against Alexander Campbell, one of the prosecutors, who also happened to have been Crittendon's law partner. By nature, presumption of guilt is the purview of the prosecution. The state's case was aided substantially by the fact Miss Fair shot Crittendon in a public place in front of numerous witnesses.

Which was likely the reason her attorney's strategy combined blame-the-victim and a temporary insanity plea. But not your common, "the cad had it coming, she snapped and let him have it." The defense hoped to prove delayed menstruation, a tipped uterus, or both, caused episodic mania and that Fair was in a hormonal fugue when she pulled the trigger.

Her lawyer maintained, with seven years' worth of opportunities to kill Crittendon by myriad means and absent witnesses, would a *sane* woman dispatch the rogue in broad daylight at a ferry landing?

Prosecutor Campbell countered that women were dangerous sexual creatures who'd run totally amok if not for the moral constraints inherent in a civilized society. Laura Fair, in his opinion, was a wanton seductress whose actions could be the result of sexual excess.

Established medical theory lent credence to both sides. Published over a decade after Laura Fair's trial, the *Homeopathic Practice of Medicine: History, Diagnosis and Treatment of Diseases in General, Including Those Peculiar to Females and the Management of Children* states that "females are far more subject to the different forms of insanity than males" adding delicately, "which is reasonable to suppose in consequence . . . of certain physical conditions that in many instances act as exciting causes, which males are not subject to."

Specifically, "sorrow, hatred, jealousy, excessive joy, disappointed love, and betrayed confidence" and "it appears from tabular reports that grief, want, and disappointed love, are by far the most frequent exciting causes."

Various menses-related segments warn of "derangement of the nervous system," "immoderate use of highly seasoned dishes," and "inordinate sexual indulgence." Suggested treatments were doses of nux-vomica (a strychnine derivative), belladonna (aka deadly nightshade), or aconite, a poison commonly known as monk's hood.

The section devoted to "uterine dropsy" is brief and mentions diagnostic fallibility, probably due to the symptoms being exclusively external, and/or determined by a patient's verbal complaints: dry skin, impaired appetite, increased thirst, and "a small, irritable pulse."

During Miss Fair's trial, it's safe to say the judge, jury, and courtroom spectators squirmed as a parade of medical experts for the prosecution and defense took the stand to share their thoughts and theories regarding menstruation.

During cross-examination, Prosecutor Campbell demolished one doctor's credibility and maneuvered another into admitting Miss Fair's symptoms could be attributed to sexual excess. By inference, when the deceased was away, his mistress played the field.

The defense read aloud over a hundred "intimate love letters" written by Crittendon to Miss Fair and vice versa. The tactic was surely designed to prove that Crittendon's false promises induced the aforementioned exciting causes, thus compromised her sanity.

Campbell's rebuttal allowed that any menstrual abnormalities and temporary dementia Fair suffered resulted from entering the business world (owning the boardinghouse) in defiance of Victorian convention. In other words, women who dare run with the big dogs (men) knowingly set themselves up for mental and physical consequences.

On the stand, Laura Fair testified that she often experienced blackouts. She recalled little of the day of Crittendon's murder, other than hearing Mrs. Crittendon's voice (in probable full scream). Admitting to periods of cognitive disability was probably an attempt to encourage reasonable doubt about her sanity, as well as the confession made upon her arrest.

On December 1, 1870, Miss Laura Fair, clad in funereal black, was found guilty of murder. If gender wasn't a factor in her conviction, it definitely didn't affect the punishment meted out. With a bang of the gavel, the judge sentenced Laura to hang.

Justice served, by Prosecutor Campbell's lights. His ridicule of her defense averred that the accused believed in free love, as did her suffragette cheering section. And if a dropped uterus and finicky menses provoked insanity, a third of San Francisco's population were potential killers.

Laura's mother, Lisle Lester, and the small, devoted band of suffragettes who attended the trial squeezed into the carriage with the convicted murderess for the ride back to prison. Because Laura had become violent and threatened suicide while awaiting trial, the group of supporters feared she'd die by her own hand before the appointment with the hangman.

According to an Internet newspaper archive, a squib dated the succeeding day read: "Mrs. Laura Fair, who recently shot and killed A. P. Crittendon on the Oakland boat, and who is now confined in the San Francisco County Jail on a charge [conviction] of murder, is very low with inflamation [sic] of the brain."

The *San Francisco Examiner* didn't question the jurors' verdict, but criticized the sentence: ". . . no man who reverences the memory of a mother can contemplate with other feelings than horror, the hanging of a woman."

Forced to remain silent during the proceedings, the feminists rallied, bolstered and emboldened by Elizabeth Cady

Stanton's and Susan B. Anthony's participation in a statewide suffragette convention. After Miss Anthony visited Laura Fair's jail cell, she was quoted as saying, "The treatment of this woman is an outrage and a disgrace to the city of San Francisco . . . If all men had protected all women as their own wives and daughters, you would have no Laura Fair in your jail tonight."

It's a shame no score was kept of the double standards ricocheting in all directions. The prosecution racked up its share, as did the defense; then suffragettes demanding legislative gender equality chastised San Francisco's male population for not safeguarding their womenfolk.

In her address to the convention, Miss Anthony's remarks about the Laura Fair trial received hisses and boos from the assembled sisterhood, which the newspapers rather gleefully recounted. She and Mrs. Stanton promptly repaired from San Francisco, only to learn speaking engagements in other towns had been cancelled. "The shadow of the newspapers hung over us," said Miss Anthony.

Public sentiment didn't find in favor of Laura Fair, but the California Supreme Court noted a technical error in the proceedings and ordered a retrial. Some sources cite improper submission of evidence; others that the higher court objected to a "guilty due to insanity" verdict.

Again the sensational case received national attention. After sixty-five hours of deliberation, the second jury voted for acquittal.

Did Laura Fair get away with the murder of Alexander Crittendon? Could she have contributed to those mysterious circumstances surrounding her first husband's death? And what about Husband Number Three's self-inflicted gun-shot?

Whatever she did, or didn't do, Laura Fair's notoriety as a "Black Widow" clung like a foul odor for the rest of her life. Few, if any, mourned her passing in 1919.

8

HENRIETTA GREEN

Never . . . give anyone anything, even for a kindness.

A fool and his money are soon parted, or so the adage goes. Henrietta "Hetty" Howland Robinson Green was no fool about money or much else. She not only hung on to the money she inherited, she parlayed it into a cool hundred million dollars.

A million in cash and another four in a trust fund might seem like a sizable head start on becoming the richest woman in the world, except plenty of family fortunes larger than Hetty's have been squandered in a single generation.

Having lost a son in infancy, her parents, Edward Mott Robinson and Abby Howland Robinson (her forebears dating back to the *Mayflower*), were again hoping for an heir, when Hetty was born on November 24, 1834.

Edward probably didn't conceal his disappointment then, and surely didn't later, as his daughter was aware of it at a young age. The blue-eyed, fair-skinned little girl couldn't change her gender, so she divined other ways to prove herself an asset to her father rather than a liability.

Her parents, devout Quakers, lived frugally despite their combined wealth derived from the whaling industry and foreign trade. Their home in New Bedford, Massachusetts, was not of the sprawling, Vanderbilt persuasion maintained by a small army of servants. In keeping with their religious beliefs, the Robinsons epitomized Spartan in all things, from meals to material objects.

Whether or not Edward realized it at the time, Hetty didn't love to tag along with him to the docks, just because her mother was often unwell. While he went about his business, his daughter listened . . . and learned.

By age five, when her father and paternal grandfather were losing their sight, Hattie read the financial section of the newspapers aloud to them. Within a year, she'd grasped what all those words and numbers meant.

Nickels given her by family members weren't frittered away on candy and geegaws, or collected in a piggy bank. Hetty deposited hers in a savings account. Later, a different lesson in "waste not, want not" was learned at school, when she turned up her nose at the food she was served. At the next meal, the same plate was set in front of her. Again, she refused to eat. On its third appearance, she swallowed her stubbornness—and the contents of her plate.

Culinary conflicts aside, formal education wasn't her forte. It's said she didn't make friends easily, and the curricula of private girls' schools of that era stressed ladylike comportment and household management, not high finance and diversification.

Conventional (male) wisdom held that women were too impulsive and simultaneously too cautious to entrust with more than pin money. Edward Robinson was either the exception to that mind-set, or resigned himself to Hetty's role as heir apparent, for at thirteen, she was keeping the books for the family business.

The job likely didn't pay much, since nepotism can be more profitable for the parent than the child. Whatever Hetty earned didn't join the nickels in her savings account. This time, she invested in the bonds market.

Legend holds that on her twenty-first birthday, she didn't light the candles on her cake, thinking it wasteful. The frosting was wiped off and the candles returned to the store for a refund. If true, the anecdote typifies the penny-pinching she'd eventually be famous for. And before she turned twenty-two, she inherited the aforementioned five million from her parents' estate, plus another sixty-five thousand from her maternal aunt's.

Trouble was, the latter was $1,935,000 shy of the bequest her aunt had promised. Hetty filed a lawsuit contesting the will and submitted a second naming her the sole beneficiary, which she swore her aunt had dictated on her death bed.

The case dragged on five years before a judge declared Hetty's handwritten will a forgery. Striking out in court on her first try created a litigious Frankenstein's monster. Over the next half-century, she filed hundreds of lawsuits and won, by settlement or decree, more than she lost.

A young woman as pretty and smart as Hetty needn't be an heiress to attract suitors. But was it her money they were courting, or her? The safest deterrent to falling for a fortune-hunter was marrying a man with his own six-figure net worth.

At thirty-three, she wed Edward Henry Green, a native of Vermont and millionaire in his own right. Love may be blind, but Hetty had the foresight to insist on the 1867 equivalent of a prenuptial agreement to ensure their respective funds remained separate.

Their son, Ned (Edward Howland Robinson Green), and daughter, Sylvia, were born in London, where the Greens resided for several years. Hetty applied her credo "Buy cheap and sell dear, act with thrift and shrewdness and be persistent" to snapping up depreciated post–Civil War government bonds. Simplistic as that philosophy was, Hetty's instinct for when to buy and when to unload was almost infallible.

In 1874, the Green family returned to the States and settled in New York City. For someone who read newspaper financial pages when most children hadn't gotten a handle on their ABC's, being within streetcar-range of Wall Street was akin to being a pilgrim in Mecca.

The timing was almost surely Hetty's idea. In the fall of the previous year, the Union Pacific railroad had spent over fifteen million dollars laying a mere five hundred miles of track. Financier Jay Cooke's failure to float a $100 million bond issue triggered a financial panic. Banks failed. Businesses couldn't meet their payrolls. Factories couldn't pay for raw materials, much less collect on due bills. Unemployment soared; property values and stock prices plummeted.

Hetty shunned the stock market, somewhat for the reasons

financier Henry Clews postulated. He chauvinistically insisted that women were too impressionable and jumped to conclusions "by a kind of instinct" or "inspiration." Which, Hetty knew, was precisely how male investors decided which stocks to buy and when to trade or sell. Essentially, the stock market was a giant, whimsical rumor mill both genders would be wiser to avoid.

"I don't believe much in stocks," she said. "I never buy industrials. Railroads and real estate are the things I like. Before deciding on an investment I seek out every kind of information about it."

And oh, how she loved a panic. Living in its epicenter was like presiding over a giant Monopoly board with oodles of cash at her disposal, and choice, undervalued properties getting cheaper by the day.

High-class bonds were another favorite, and she'd learned the magic of compound interest from all those nickels saved in her childhood bank account. While the so-called robber barons built palaces on Fifth Avenue, lit imported cigars with hundred-dollar bills, and showered their wives and mistress with diamonds, Hetty Green methodically turned five million dollars into twenty-six million in less than thirty years.

Unfortunately, Edward was neither as financially conservative nor risk-averse as his wife. Then, as now, speculators can leverage a few million into a billion overnight. Or, like Edward Green, wind up with a gold pocketwatch, seven bucks in a money-clip, and several zeroes in the hole.

In Hetty's opinion, he'd committed several deadly sins. Speculating on anything was the antithesis of frugality, which was as natural to her as breathing. Debt was an abomination.

Interest was to be earned, not paid. And perhaps worst of all, she had to cover the shortfall.

"My husband is of no use to me at all," she said, having shown Edward the door and slammed it permanently behind him. "I wish I did not have him. He is a burden to me."

Benjamin Franklin, America's best-known and oft-quoted Quaker, averred, "A penny saved is a penny earned." Contemporary money-management gurus espouse, "Save more, spend less" to readers, watchers, and listeners who think, *Easier said than done.*

Not, of course, for Hetty Green. Spending less wasn't good enough. An intellectual challenge, a sense of triumph stemmed from spending as little as possible. Her notorious, obsessive parsimony earned her the title "world's greatest miser" in *Guinness Book of Records*, even though by definition, a miser sacrifices creature comforts to sustain his monetary hoard. Sacrifice Hetty did, as did her two children by default. Except a true hoarder wouldn't have lent millions (via municipal bonds) to the City of New York—one of countless other savvy and lucrative mortgages held nationwide.

Examples of her stinginess abound. The most infamous was refusing to take son Ned to a doctor when he dislocated his knee. Not because she was cold-hearted and cruel—she adored both her children. Like most moms, she probably believed her medical skills rivaled a doctor's, particularly well before university-trained physicians were the norm.

When his condition worsened, she and Ned, dressed in rags, joined the queue at a charity clinic. The doctor, recognizing her and demanding a fee-for-services, affirmed her bizarre contention that the wealthy were penalized for their success; ergo, if the destitute received free medical care, why should the rich have to pay?

A blue-blooded capitalist favoring socialized medicine was rarer than a degreed M.D. In the end, Ned paid the price for his mother's stinginess: his by-then gangrenous leg had to be amputated.

To an interviewer's question regarding philanthropy, Hetty said, "You never saw my name on a charity [donor] list, did you? But I built whole blocks of buildings in Chicago when the workingmen had to have employment."

The Witch of Wall Street didn't ride a flying broom, but did dress the part: tattered, unrelieved black skirts, dresses, and bonnets that gradually took on a shiny, greenish cast from age and constant wear.

In her voluminous petticoats, she sewed deep pockets large enough to hold the contents of a safe-deposit box or, in at least one instance, $200,000 worth of negotiable bonds.

The chain around her waist strung with hundreds of safety deposit box keys jangled when she walked. Come winter, a rustling sound emanated from thermal unmentionables fashioned from newspapers.

Nor did Hetty smell fresh as a daisy, most days. Small wonder, as she usually laundered just the lower "street-sweeper" portion of her skirts. And in part, perhaps, because of the baked onions she chewed, believing them the secret to good health and longevity.

Almost daily, she went to her "office" at Chemical National Bank. Stashed under a staircase near the vault were assorted trunks and bags that contained reams of financial documents and served as a makeshift desk and seat. In that dim nook near the vault, Hetty clipped coupons from piles of bonds, the ink blackening her hands and fingers. At lunchtime, she either fished an unwrapped ham sandwich from a petticoat pocket or warmed a bowl of oatmeal on the radiator.

Property taxes were one of many banes of her existence. For decades, to avoid establishing a permanent residence, she'd circuit from one cheap boardinghouse to another, zigzagging every other night or so between the Bowery, Harlem, Hoboken, and Brooklyn.

Dewey, her dog's name, was one of many pseudonyms she registered under. The tactic backfired (almost) in New Jersey, when someone recognized her and tipped the authorities that she owned an unlicensed dog. Rather than pay the two-dollar fee, Hetty scuttled back to New York and stayed at a friend's apartment for a few days.

In his book, *The Day They Shook the Plum Tree*, biographer Arthur Lewis excoriates her lifestyle and business practices: "The fortune [inheritance] . . . became gigantic in the hands of Hetty Green . . . through forgery, perjury, ruthlessness and financial genius . . ." He further called her a "nomadic tax dodger by night and a busy money lender by day."

Aware of her detractors' low opinions of her, but unperturbed, she said, "My life is written for me down in Wall Street by people who, I assume, do not care to know one iota of the real Hetty Green. I am in earnest; therefore they picture me heartless. I go my own way, take no partners, risk nobody else's fortune, therefore I am Madame Ishmael, set against every man."

The good and rich old boys network's disdain notwithstanding, Hetty's daughter, Sylvia, married Matthew Wilks, John Jacob Astor's grandson. Ned was given the responsibility of managing his mother's extensive real estate investments in Chicago. Telegraphed instructions he received were never signed, but Ned never questioned whether Hetty had sent them, as all were sent collect.

Each month, he wired forty thousand dollars in rents to his mother in exchange for a six-dollar salary—which was cut in half when Hetty realized her son was skimming a few bucks off the top.

In 1892, she put him in charge of negotiating the purchase of a fifty-eight-mile section of the Houston and Texas Central Railway. The deal included a quarter-million acres of land and a franchise to extend the railway to the Red River.

Outbidding Texas railroad man Collings P. Huntington made a powerful and permanent enemy. Hetty then purchased another span between Garrett and Roberts, Texas, and consolidated the whole shebang into the Texas Midland Railroad, naming Ned as president.

The ensuing litigation between Huntington and the Greens probably wasn't profitable for anyone other than their respective attorneys. Huntington eventually recovered the original property, but the wrangling continued for several years.

On July 3, 1916, the Witch of Wall Street died at the ripe old age of 81. According to one source, the cause was apoplexy triggered by an argument over the virtues of canned milk. Another alludes to a prior series of strokes and her confinement to a wheelchair.

In any event, the woman who used to buy her children broken cookies at the grocery store to save a few pennies left them an estate valued at over one hundred million dollars (approximately two billion, in today's dollars).

Shortly after the funeral, Ned married the former prostitute he'd kept on the payroll as a housekeeper for twenty-four years. He then sank a million dollars in the renovation of a 225-foot steamship. His fascination with "the miracle of radio" led to a donation to Dartmouth College to build and equip the most cutting-edge station in the country at the time.

In 1930, his and Sylvia's combined contributions financed Hetty Green Hall at Wellesley College. Hetty's daughter also donated millions to a variety of civic and charitable organizations, including several hospitals.

Sylvia, who survived her brother and husband but had no children, bequeathed the balance of her mother's enormous fortune to friends, relatives, and institutions.

In 1998, *American Heritage* magazine compiled a list of the forty richest Americans in history based on 1998 dollars. Only one woman made the list: Henrietta Howland Green.

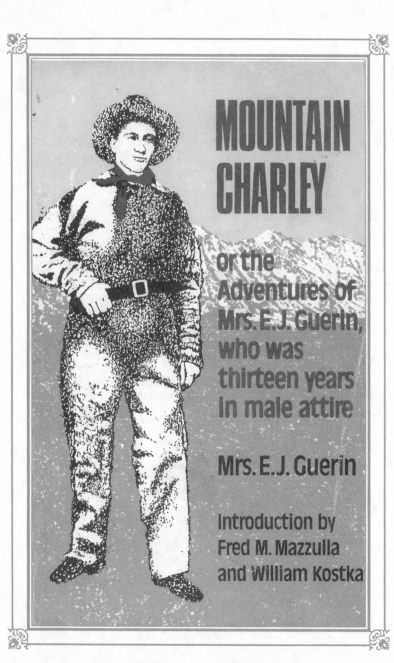

MOUNTAIN CHARLEY

or the Adventures of Mrs. E. J. Guerin, who was thirteen years in male attire

Mrs. E. J. Guerin

Introduction by Fred M. Mazzulla and William Kostka

9

ELSA JANE GUERIN

I emptied my revolver upon him as he lay, and should have done the same with its mate had not two hunters at that moment come upon the ground and prevented any further consummation of my designs.

The autobiography given in the following pages is literal actual fact, except so far as the conversations and incidents of one or two dramatic scenes. . . ." So says the preface to E. J. (Elsa Jane) Guerin's self-published memoirs.

If so, the Southern belle born around 1837 packed adventures enough for two lifetimes into one, complete with a second wardrobe befitting her male alter ego, Charley Forest.

"My life passed without much variation till I reached the age of twelve years," she wrote, "at which time an event occurred that had a marked bearing on my whole life."

The event to which she refers is a clandestine romance with "a gentleman whose appearance pleased me," while she attended a private school in New Orleans. After her *Romeo and*

Juliet-style (and perhaps inspired) clamber out a window and into her beau's waiting arms, the couple found a minister willing to pronounce them man and wife.

Though Elsa Jane never mentions her beloved's name, the newlyweds took a honeymoon tour through the South, then settled in St. Louis, Missouri.

The husband's job piloting a Mississippi riverboat meant extended absences from home, but Elsa Jane was quite content to keep house and wait for his return. They soon were blessed with a son and later, a daughter.

Tragedy struck when Elsa Jane's second child was only three months old. The stranger who appeared on Elsa Jane's doorstep said her husband had scuffled with a crew member named Jamieson and been shot to death.

Elsa Jane was devastated emotionally and financially. Her husband's wages had paid the bills, with nothing left over. A collection taken by his fellow Masons paid for the funeral and burial. The remainder was given to Elsa Jane, but it wasn't enough to sustain a sixteen-year-old widow with two small children for long.

Uppermost in her mind was divining a way to support herself, her toddler son, and her infant daughter and someday, somehow exacting revenge on the man who'd murdered her husband.

"At length, after casting over in my mind everything that presented itself as a remedy, I determined upon a project. . . . I was to dress myself in male attire, and seek for a living in this disguise among the avenues which are so religiously closed against my sex."

Elsa Jane was neither the first nor last to try to pass as a man for economic reasons. Countless other women disguised their gender to protect themselves and their virtue. Patriotic fervor, or a refusal to sit home while their sweethearts or husbands marched off to war, added several females masquerading as males to the rank and file.

Before Elsa Jane's transformation to Charley Forest, she placed her children in the care of the Sisters of Charity. Her long hair was shorn and she practiced lowering her voice, already a trifle hoarse from an "asthmatic infection" dating back to her tenure at the New Orleans finishing school. Her language coarsened and gestures she observed were mimicked, as the gender less likely to be fooled by her disguise was the one she'd adopted.

Several test runs in daylight and after dark raised no curious looks or inquiries. In the manner of what you see being what you get, those she encountered saw and accepted her as a boy in middle teens:

> I found myself able to banish almost wholly, the woman from my countenance. I buried my sex in my heart and roughened the surface so that the grave would not be discovered—as men on the plains *cache* some treasure, and build a fire over the spot so that the charred embers may hide the secret.

Not as successful were her first attempts at finding work. Why isn't explained, but making the acquaintance of "River men" led to a cabin boy's job on a steamer. Probably, having been married to a pilot, Elsa Jane was familiar with the jargon and may well have attributed shipboard anecdotes and incidents he'd experienced to young Charley Forest.

Every month, Charley reverted to Elsa Jane for visitations with her children. Not referenced is how she explained her mannish hairstyle. Back then, a woman's crowning glory was intricately curled, waved, upswept, coiled, braided, thickened with dyed horsehair switches, bejeweled, and beflowered.

A coal-scuttle bonnet might have been employed, but never removing it would surely have seemed odd to the nuns, as well as to Elsa Jane's children.

After four years on the river, Elsa Jane/Charley became a brakeman for the Illinois Central Railroad. Trains usually had two "brakies," one riding atop a front car and the other at the back. At the engineer's whistle, the brakies turned a mechanism (resembling a steering wheel attached to a driveshaft) jutting up from each car, leaping from one to the next, working toward each other.

In pitch darkness, rain, sleet, subzero cold, the jumps between swaying, jostling cars were "wing and a prayer" maneuvers that sent many a brakie to that big railyard in the sky.

In time, a conductor who apparently divined that Charley the brakie wasn't of the masculine persuasion conspired with a confederate to ply Charley with liquor over dinner, then rape her. Upon hearing their plot, she feigned intoxication, made an excuse to leave the table, and ran for her lodgings. A carpetbag stuffed with her possessions and a dash to a steamer bound for Detroit effected her escape.

A circuitous return to St. Louis via Niagra Falls "and other places of interest along the route" allowed her a joyous reunion with her children, but "although I had resumed my womanly dress and habits, I could not wholly eradicate many of the tastes which I had acquired during my life as one of the stronger sex."

Charley larked about the city, meandering about the wharves, partaking of the entertainments her guise afforded at saloons, theaters, and gambling houses. While leisurely people-watching at the King's Hotel, she recognized then followed her husband's killer, barely containing her rage and need to exact justice.

This segment of her memoirs contains the first mention of Charley's holstered sidearm (which wasn't as common an accoutrement as books, Hollywood, and television depict). She must have practiced fast-draws along with walking and talking like a man, for she told Jamieson who she was, thumbed the pistol's hammer, and jerked the trigger.

And missed, as did he. Her second shot drilled Jamieson's shoulder. His snapped her thighbone. Both wounded, but neither mortally, each staggered off in opposite directions before the authorities arrived at the scene.

A six-month recuperation, she avers, left "a considerable hole . . . in my finances." Precluded by, one assumes, a whopper of a cover story to explain how a young widow and mother of two dressed as a boy sustained a gunshot wound to the leg.

Because the job market for women hadn't changed a bit during the intervening years, in early 1855, Elsa Jane returned her children to the Sisters of Charity, freeing Charley Forest to join a prospecting expedition to California. "If I met with ordinary success," she wrote, ". . . I could retire into more private life, resume my proper dress, and thereafter in company with my children enjoy life to the full extent that circumstances would permit."

The autobiography reproduces the journal Charley kept during the trek west. Landmarks noted and descriptions of the terrain, both majestic and bleak, jibe with the wagon trains' ofttimes arduous journey. However what's left out piques considerable curiosity.

Victorian delicacy notwithstanding, it's plausible that Charley's employ as a cabin boy and a brakie might have afforded enough privacy for female-specific ablutions. Traveling overland, particularly in regions where, say, convenient stands of shrubbery are few and days between, would seriously complicate, if not compromise, her masquerade.

In addition, while a neckerchief would disguise the telltale absence of an Adam's apple, it would be fascinating to know how she diverted suspicion about a dearth of facial hair. Did she pretend to shave every morning? Divine some disease, or quirky medical anomaly?

However she skirted that issue, the sojourn to California didn't pan out quite the way Charley anticipated. Gold-prospecting being more grueling and less profitable than gold-earning, Charley went to work in a Sacramento saloon. Somehow, on a hundred-dollar monthly salary and despite the goldfields' inflated cost of living, within six months she paid five hundred dollars for a half-interest in the saloon, with another five hundred dollars due and payable in ninety days.

Between intermittent forays to St. Louis, the enterprising Charley Forest started a pack-mule freight-hauling company to supply mountain mining camps. She also allegedly drove a cattle herd from Missouri to her California ranch to fatten them up before their sale.

Selling out all her businesses reaped a thirty-thousand-dollar profit. In the late 1850s, it should have provided a fine roof over her family's head for decades at a time when a thousand-dollar annual income was the high end of the wage scale. Instead, around 1859, Charley leased the Mountain Boy's saloon in gold-fevered Denver City.

Now known as Mountain Charley Forest, in her leisure time, the saloonkeeper enjoyed "frequent excursions to various portions of the mountains—sometimes for exercise, at others for the purpose of prospecting, or to visit some sick miner."

Astride a mule and some three miles from civilization, she spied a rider approaching, also on muleback. Proximity revealed him to be none other than the blackguard Jamieson. Charley's aim having improved over the years, she shot him out of the saddle, emptied one revolver into his prostrate form, and would have cut loose with the other if not for the two hunters drawn to the site by the shots.

Jamieson miraculously survived, only to expire months later in New Orleans from yellow fever. However, before he departed Denver City, he "told the whole story of my past life so far as he knew it and exculpated me wholly for the attempts on his life."

Announcing that Mountain Charley Forest was actually a woman is believable. Being shot in the shoulder in St. Louis, then surviving multiple ventilation in Denver City, yet declaring bygones-be-bygones strains credulity beyond the breaking point.

Elsa Jane abruptly concludes her memoirs by stating she wed her bartender, H. L. Guerin, subsequently moved to St. Joseph, Missouri, "where my husband now resides," adding, "My children are at school in Georgia."

Since the book's original printing in 1861, skepticism abounds regarding which parts reflect the preface's "literal actual fact" and which "one or two dramatic scenes" are the exceptions.

Further complicating the bona fides is the fact that another cross-dressing female known as Charley Parkhurst (aka Charlotte Darkey Parkhurst) had several experiences similar to Charley Forest's. Significantly different was that Parkhurst's true gender wasn't revealed until a coroner's postmortem examination.

As if two legendary Charleys traipsing around Colorado Territory weren't enough, a third Mountain Charley (also Christian-named Charlotte) who *didn't* disguise her gender supposedly served as Charles Hatfield in the Iowa Cavalry during the Civil War.

So which—or who—was the *real* Mountain Charley? Did Elsa Jane Guerin create a composite of the others and self-publish it as her own memoir?

The University of Oklahoma Press's new edition published in 1968 contains an editorial introduction that states the landmarks and trail markers in Guerin's journal section seem genuine: "The places mentioned, misspelled as they often were in those days, still exist." Hence, if Elsa Jane confabulated the entire story, it's likely she'd have used the landmarks' proper spelling, not compounded the errors.

Although a journal entry also purports that Charley Forest saw the Great Salt Lake from a distance of *seventy-five miles*, Denver City *was* home to a Mountain Boy's saloon at the time Charley/Elsa Jane allegedly owned it.

It's said that autobiography is the sincerest form of fiction. Intentional or not, memory is fickle at best and flawed by accident and design.

From a novelist's perspective, educated guesswork suggests that Guerin's book is about one-half true, a quarter some shade thereof, and a fourth pure balderdash.

Besides the journal segment's veracity, other scenes "feel" genuine, rather than a breezy means to an end. An incident similar to the rape attempt, for example, may have happened to

Elsa Jane, which she reiterated in the guise of railroad brake-man, Charley Forest. If so, casting a conductor as the predator was a logical choice.

Just as plausibly, the scene could be a nod to melodramas of the era whereby Fair Lady's virtue is threatened, but by pluck and luck, she escapes the villain's clutches. Chances are, elements of each are at work, with Elsa Jane either missing or dismissing the complications (and implications) of a boy as prey, instead of a girl.

To the contrary, in no respect are Charley's shoot-outs with arch-nemesis Jamieson believable—the second, in particular. As clear as the ink on the page is the author's reluctance to kill off Jamieson, fearing readers would be appalled by a woman (Charley persona or no) exacting delayed frontier justice. Opting for Jamieson's last-minute rescue, then blowing Charley's cover but affecting mutual redemption by forgiving her is an eye-roller—even without quasi-biblical retribution via Jamieson's fatal case of yellow fever.

Whether true, partly true, or a flight of Elsa Jane Guerin's literary fancy, if she hoped fame and fortune would result from the book's 1861 printing, she was sorely disappointed. By 1953, only one copy of her original work was known to exist.

As Louis L'Amour expressed in *The Walking Drum,* perhaps a simpler, personal motivation guided Guerin's pen: "... I wanted a life wider and deeper than my own ... To make my way in a larger world, to see more, to learn more, to be more. This was my dream."

(Library of Congress, LC-USZ62-64301)

10

FRANCES BENJAMIN
JOHNSTON

*Learn early the immense difference between the photograph
that is merely a photograph, and that which is also a picture.*

The term *photojournalist* didn't enter the dictionary until
about 1938—about the time Frances Benjamin Johnston
retired from being one for more than fifty years.

Even before her interest in art veered away from brushes,
canvases, and palettes to images captured on calotype (paper-
negative photography), Frances firmly believed one's private
life should remain private.

A sketch of her own life remains of the thumbnail variety.
With few exceptions (*A Talent for Detail*, by Pete Daniel and
Raymond Smock, a comprehensive source of quoted material),
biographers have largely ignored Miss Johnston as subject matter.

The woman who would someday wield a camera "with unblinking honesty" was born in Grafton, West Virginia, on January 15, 1864. From there, her childhood homes ranged from the Ohio River to Rochester, New York, and Washington, D.C.

A clue to her ancestry was her mother's and her membership in the Daughters of the American Revolution. A familial dustup must have occurred several generations back, since Frances's great-great-grandfather fought for the British.

Her art studies began at Notre Dame Convent in Govanstan, Maryland. At the age of nineteen, she traveled to Paris and spent two years training at the Academi Julien. Returning to the United States in 1885, she entered another art school, but her interest was on the wane.

While working as a freelance newspaper illustrator, she gradually realized that photography-as-journalism was the wave of the future. By its name, photography means "writing with light" and was, as she noted, "a more accurate medium" than traditional artistic expression.

Her perception and timing were spot-on. From Leonardo da Vinci to Joseph Nicephore Niépce's experiments in 1816 to Louis Daguerre's glass plate daguerreotypes, the fascination with and challenges of reproducing fixed images had proceeded inchmeal for centuries until William Henry Fox Talbot's negative-positive method of producing photographs on paper.

The paper, treated with glycerin and castor oil, was rolled into a reel for loading into the camera. After exposure, negative images were immersed in hot water to dissolve the gelatin, then chemically "fixed."

The process enabled Eastman Kodak Company's founder, George Eastman, to market his revolutionary Kodak camera to professionals and amateurs alike. Compared to the large, cumbersome "wet-plate" cameras and equipment Matthew Brady transported by wagon during the Civil War, Eastman's Kodak was about the size of a wooden shoebox. A drop-down door supported the accordion-like bellows and lens mechanism.

Eastman's slogan, "You push the button, we do the rest," was literal and reminiscent of today's disposable camera processing. Priced at twenty-five dollars (not cheap, but a Sears, Roebuck single-plate stereoscopic model was over seventy-five dollars) the Kodak came preloaded with a one hundred-exposure reel. Once used, the camera and a ten-dollar fee were sent to Eastman headquarters in Rochester, New York. The film was developed and the prints, negatives, and reloaded camera were then returned by mail.

Frances Johnston spent some portion of her childhood in Rochester, so it's possible she or her parents were acquainted with George Eastman. In any event, to her inquiry regarding a camera suitable for press photography, he sent a Kodak with his compliments.

Armed with the tools of her emerging trade, Frances studied for a while under Thomas Smillie, head of the Smithsonian's Division of Photography. She was either an A+ pupil, or an early disciple of the "film is cheap; learn by doing" school, for her first photos appeared in the December 1889 issue of *Demorest's Family Magazine.*

The photographs, taken at the U.S. Mint, were accompanied by an article Johnston wrote in a style as clear and professional as her photos. Before long and probably due to time constraints, she ceased providing prose with her pictures.

The Kohinoor Mines in Shenandoah City, Pennsylvania, was Johnston's next assignment for *Demorest's.* Forewarning from the editor about the combustibility of magnesium flash powder for illumination didn't daunt Miss Johnston one iota.

According to *A Talent For Detail*, four grueling hours' work netted only three acceptable negatives at a site where "everything was so hopelessly black, excepting the blank white reflections caught on the polished surfaces of the coal."

The miners' quarters above-ground weren't significantly brighter than below: "As a matter of course," she said, "everything and everybody is black. Great, unsightly frame buildings—the coal breakers—dingy with dirt and clum, while the small cottages and rude wooden shanties of the miners cluster drearily about the outskirts."

What became as much a part of her photographic technique as the camera itself, she then talked with the miners and their families and visited their homes. Later, from documenting female shoe factory workers to cigar-box makers, Frances acquainted herself with her subjects, rather than just point, shoot, and scram.

A critic later remarked, Miss Johnston "is of no particular school or class. She follows no traditions and no rules." Other than her own, which was to respect and abide by her instincts. In addition, she observed,

> The woman who makes photography profitable must have, as to personal qualities, good common sense, unlimited patience to carry her through endless failures, equally unlimited tact, good taste, a quick eye, a talent for detail, and a genius for hard work.

In her case, a business manager might have been helpful, as well. Although she maintained, "I have not been able to lose sight of the pecuniary side, though for the sake of money or anything else I would never publish a photograph which fell below the standard I have set for myself," she was often so caught up in a project, she neglected to open her bills, let alone pay them promptly.

Blessed (or cursed) with boundless energy, she slept little, wakened early, and sometimes forgot to submit prints for a completed project before barreling off on a new assignment, a trip, or an adventure.

By the early 1890s, using her parents' bathroom as a makeshift darkroom had become an inconvenience for all concerned. What the elder Johnstons thought of the two-story studio Frances built behind their house isn't known, but visitors surely didn't mistake it for a carriage-house.

The building's sharp angles, clean lines, pitched façade, and twelve-by-sixteen-foot slanted skylight couldn't have been more atypical of Victorian architecture had Frank Lloyd Wright drafted the blueprints.

The interior was spacious but cozy. Functional yet comfortable. Uncluttered—another antithesis of the era's excesses—but filled with assorted personal treasures: from German beer steins to primitives to powder horns.

Linquist Robert William Chapman said, "A house is infinitely communicative, and tells many things besides the figure of its master's income." If so, Frances's studio conveys the two distinct sides of her personality. In essence, she was a genteel Victorian lady in an unconventional, male-dominated profession who enjoyed a glass of bourbon before dinner and socialized with actors, writers, and artists.

A straitlaced Bohemian, as it were—a contradiction she ac-

knowledged in two self-portraits. The photos have been inter-
preted as a mockery of Victorian convention, except Frances
wasn't a suffragette, crusader, or social reformer. Because she
said, "In portraiture, especially, there are so many possibilities
for picturesque effects—involving composition, light and
shade, the study of pose, the arrangement of drapery...,"
perhaps the pictures were merely a lark and photographic experiment combined.

And she constantly experimented, though she kept her dis-
coveries tucked under her fashionable hat. For example, unlike
the coal mine photographs, shots taken at Mammoth Cave,
Kentucky, showed a marked improvement in composition.
When *Demorest's* editor asked about her technique, she wrote
back, "As to the difficulties, disasters, but ultimate triumph ...
when I sought to vanquish the arch-enemy darkness with
flashpowder, it is too long a story."

In 1898, she was among the first photographers hired by
George G. Bain's fledgling Montauk Photo Concern in New
York City. For a thirty- to sixty-dollar syndication fee, newspapers received eight photos a day from Montauk. In addition,
clients were required to supply Bain with their local- and
human-interest photos—the genesis of file photo archives still
used today.

One of Bain's assignments coincided with commissions
Frances had already secured in Paris. That city was among Ad-
miral George Dewey's ports of call en route to the United
States. Bain was champing for current photographs of the hero
of Manila Bay.

"Get Dewey, Dewey, Dewey!" were his exact instructions,
adding that he'd sent a second photographer, J. C. Hemment

and that he'd heard Hemment's ethics were a tad wobbly. The ace up Frances's French-cuffed sleeve was a letter of introduction from friend and assistant Secretary of the Navy, Theodore Roosevelt. And being a charming, attractive woman didn't hurt.

She toured the *Olympia* forecastle to fantail, the bridge and below ships, talking to swabbies, taking photographs, (some 150 in all), asking questions, and repairing to the torpedo room to reload her camera's plate-holders. Dinner was taken in the crew's mess, where she filled out an enlistment record, listing her trade as "snapshots." From seamanship to marksmanship, she rated herself a topnotch 5. In sobriety, she gave herself a 4.9.

Three weeks later, George Bain was having conniptions. He'd received Hemment's photos (which the photog was secondary-marketing like hotcakes), but hadn't received a telegram from Frances, let alone her pictures. It seems Hemment had very kindly offered to have her negatives developed with his. He'd posted his batch to Bain but "accidently" left Frances's in London.

Bain cabled to Frances, *WHY did you entrust your negatives to the only person who was working against you?* The question went unanswered, but all was not lost. Her photos hit print well after Hemment's and others, but exceeded theirs in quality and scope.

A commission to photograph the Washington, D.C., schools for consideration as part of the United States exhibit at the Paris Exposition dominoed into a series pivotal to her career.

To meet the six-week deadline, by day, Frances lugged cameras, tripods, and equipment from school to school, cajoling children not to move a muscle for up to a half-minute for each shot. At night, she developed and printed the negatives—a total of seven hundred interior and exterior photos.

Two in particular are evocative of Frances's artistic eye and flair for composition and detail. The first is a wide-angle photograph of schoolchildren boarding a trolley—mundane, perhaps, but Frances envisioned what the shot could become. By enlarging just the upper, windowed area of the trolley with the children looking out this way and that—some standing, some having taken their seats—the window-frames divide those images into what appears to be a series of miniature photos.

The Paris exhibit earned Frances the prestigious Palmes Académiques award. Honored as she was to receive the recognition, as anyone in the creative arts knows, awards don't put food on the table. Neither, unfortunately, did the series of booklets she produced, titled *The New Education Illustrated*.

The Washington schools' project did lead to commissions from the Hampton Institute, the Tuskegee Institute, and Carlisle Indian School. The resulting collections were at once groundbreaking and controversial in some respects. Hampton's and Tuskegee's student bodies were predominantly black, and Carlisle's was Native American—two ethnic groups many Americans believed *couldn't* be educated (read civilized), while others avidly believed they *shouldn't*.

One photograph taken at Hampton and another at the Carlisle School provide social and racial juxtaposition that Frances didn't stage, yet she couldn't have asked for a more thought-provoking example of documentary photojournalism.

In the Hampton Institute photo, a group of black children are gazing at an Indian dressed in tribal garb, complete with feathered headdress. Six months later, at the Carlisle Indian School, Frances captured a class of about twenty-five students debating the pros and cons of a topic clearly legible on an adjacent chalkboard: RESOLVED—THAT THE NEGROES OF THE SOUTH SHOULD NOT BE DENIED THE RIGHT OF CITIZENSHIP.

A year prior to the Tuskegee Institute commission, Frances's growing interest in architectural photography led her and her camera to the Pan-American Exposition in Buffalo, New York. Having for several years enjoyed an "insider's" access to the White House and First Families, she was granted a spot near the reviewing stand to listen to President William McKinley's address to the crowd.

"He was always so sweet and kind and gentle," she said, "and so anxious to pose just the way you wanted him to, but always a little self-conscious before the camera, and so never at his best. But I finally caught him at the climax of a great speech, when he had wholly forgotten himself, and it proved to be his best portrait . . ."

As well as his last. Now known as the "buffalo pose," after which his statue at the McKinley Monument in Canton, Ohio, was modeled, within minutes of Frances's photograph, McKinley was shot by alleged anarchist Leon Czolgosz and died eight days later.

The demand for Frances's photograph was enormous and spanned the globe. She sold thousands of prints, but as often as not, received no royalties for them. George Eastman's idea of kite-tailing an advertising campaign to the Number 4 Bulls-Eye Special Kodak she'd used that day apparently bowed to good taste.

The following year, in the hope of raising public awareness and funding, Booker T. Washington commissioned photographs of the Tuskegee Institute he'd founded in Alabama a decade earlier. The industrial school's work-study concept allowed students to earn tuition via educational sweat equity. Unfortunately expenses exceeded income, and few private schools survive without endowments.

Frances also wanted to document one of the outlying campuses, known as the "little Tuskegees." After taking her typical hundreds of interior and exterior shots at the main school, she traveled by train to Ramer, Alabama's so-named Colored Industrial School.

Aboard the same train was George Washington Carver, whose renown as an agricultural scientist was still ahead of him. Arriving in Ramer well after dark, Frances was met by Nelson E. Henry, principal of the school, in whose home she'd planned to stay overnight. Weary from the trip and having buggied a good distance from town before realizing her host's house was several miles farther on, she insisted he turn back for Ramer so she could check into a hotel and get some rest.

A Talent For Detail puts their time of arrival in Ramer at 11 P.M. The sole witnesses to Nelson and Frances's earlier departure and return were "Postmaster George Turnipseed's son and a 'desperado' named Armes." Incensed at the sight of a black man and a white woman buggying into the night and coming back an hour later, Armes (evidently a-slosh with liquid courage) fired several shots in Henry's general direction. In the fracas, George Washington Carver spirited Frances out of Ramer and to a hotel in a neighboring town.

Carver later called Frances ". . . the pluckiest woman I ever saw. She was not afraid for herself but shed bitter tears for Mr. Henry and for the school which is in all probability broken up."

It was, and a furious Frances Johnston descended on the Alabama capital in Montgomery. She threatened to sue Turnipseed and Armes, to have the elder Turnipseed stripped of his post office job, to sic President Theodore Roosevelt on the entire town.

The furor (hers and that of the residents of Ramer) diminished in time. Frances's eagerness to produce a permanent, visual record of Tuskegee and two satellite campuses—as well as impoverished but proud Southern black families she met while traveling the countryside—did not.

Portraiture wasn't her favorite photographic realm, yet her list of subjects reads like a historic who's who. Among them: Susan B. Anthony, Theodore Roosevelt and his wife and children, Alexander Graham Bell, Jacob Riis, Andrew Carnegie, writers Mark Twain, Richard Hovey and Neith Boyce Hapgood, and actresses Jane Cowl and Julia Marlow.

Joel Chandler Harris, famously known as Uncle Remus, was a shy man unnerved at the thought of sitting for a formal portrait. Frances's ability to put people at ease and render the camera virtually invisible, produced a portrait Harris and his wife said captured what Frances described as his "twinkle." It was reproduced on *Uncle Remus' Home Magazine's* stationery, the commemorative stamp the U.S. Postal Service issued in 1948, and the dust jacket of the Robert L. Wiggins biography, *The Life of Joel Chandler Harris.*

In 1910, Frances indulged her love of and talent for garden and architectural photography. Her client list included a number of prominent New York architects and architectural firms, as well as the Whitney estate and those of John Pierpont Morgan and John Jacob Astor.

A sideline to those specialized pursuits was an extensive speaking tour. "My lectures not only appeal to garden clubs, but also to organizations fostering civic improvement, art and literary study, in that I endeavor to present the best sources of information on a wide range of subjects relating to gardens and flowers."

The Daniel and Smock biography also credits her with being among the first women photographers (if not *the* first) to specialize in color processing. Early in her career, she kept detailed notes for later reference when hand-tinting and coloring images, a common practice before the advent of color film.

With Henry Irving, she coauthored a book titled *Colonial Churches in Virginia* (1930). Three additional books, *The Early Architecture of North Carolina* (1930), *Plantations of the Carolina Low Country* (1938), and *The Early Architecture of Georgia* (1941) were resulted from a Carnegie grant-funded tour through the South. It was said that, perusing the countryside in a chauffeur-driven car, she could "smell an old colonial house five miles off the highway."

Woodrow Wilson said, "No woman should ever be quite accurate about her age." At seventy-six, Frances was showing hers. She walked with a cane, and undoubtedly, time had clouded that sharp eye for detail. She didn't entirely retire her cameras, but the woman behind the lens bought a long-neglected house on Bourbon Street in New Orleans. The address was likely a source of amusement, for on doctor's orders, she now drank wine during cocktail hour instead of whiskey—a spirit of compromise, so to speak, of which he may not have been aware.

"I've learned not to depend on the Lord," she reportedly said. "I'll make the changes myself."

Restoring the house and courtyard garden gave yet another

creative outlet for her passion for Southern architecture and flowers. She still lectured on occasion and in 1947 traveled to the Library of Congress to donate what constituted her life's work: some 17,000 items of correspondence, 20,000 prints, and 3,700 glass and film negatives.

Though she died on March 16, 1952, her photographic legacy continues to be exhibited, reproduced, collected, and admired as both documentation of the art of photography and a historic record.

One would think her veritable bales of letters and notes would have given a clearer picture of Frances Johnston herself, but the inner woman remains an enigma. And there's nothing like an unexamined life that fosters speculation and assumptions—which Miss Johnston may have intended in a last laugh sort of a way.

Joe Elbert, who at the time of her death was assistant photography editor at the *Washington Post*, was quoted as saying, "Women [photographers] peel away the layers of a story like an artichoke; men like to slam in there, go for the money picture and move on. Of course, that is a generalization, and there are exceptions to the rule . . ."

A rule Miss Frances Benjamin Johnston intuited and adhered to nearly a century before Elbert's observation was made.

(Library of Congress, LC-USZ62-52371)

II

ADAH ISAACS MENKEN

I am lost to art and life. Yet, when all is said and done,
have I not at my age tasted more of life than most
women who live to be a hundred?

Adah Isaacs Menken was an actress, a formally trained ballerina, a literal drama queen, a published poet, a shrewd self-promotor, and a liar pretty much all her life.

Not a pathological liar or the type that tears down others to build herself up. The Menken, as she came to be known internationally, prevaricated at will and at a whim to sustain her woman-of-mystery persona. And just as she anticipated, the public—fans and foes alike—ate it up with a long-handled spoon.

Playing three-card monte with autobiographical details and the nineteenth century's less-than-comprehensive record-keeping makes her bona fides tough to nail down. Most historians agree that she was born in Louisiana in 1835, probably in Milneburg, near New Orleans.

Though some biographers assert that she was raised a Catholic, her parents, August and Marie Theodore were Jewish. Adah herself once responded to a reporter's question regarding her faith: "I was born in [Judaism], and have adhered to it through all my erratic career. Through that pure and simple religion I have found greatest comfort and blessing."

She later contributed poems and essays to the Jewish weekly newspaper, *The Israelite*, and even at the apex of her popularity, refused to perform during High Holy Days.

Discrepancies regarding her birth name being Ada, or Adah McCord, daughter of James McCord, seem improbable. She and her younger sibling(s) were billed as The Theodore Sisters at the New Orleans Opera House. Earnings from these early balletic performances were the girls' and their mother's means of support after August Theodore's death and subsequent death of Marie Theodore's second husband.

Either with her sister(s), or as soloist, Adah traveled to Cuba, becoming a favorite at the Tacon Theater. Sometime afterward, Adah was touring in Texas when she was famously and completely fictitiously rescued from a band of bloodthirsty Comanches by none other than Sam Houston. According to one account, the tall handsome Texan galloped into the fray, fired from the hip, killing seven Indians with five shots, then scooped up Adah into his arms, and vamoosed.

Houston then adopted Adah and raised the little girl destined to become the "Frenzy of 'Frisco." Variations on Adah's favorite whopper added a Comanche chief to the cast, his tomahawk aloft to scalp poor Adah, when Houston snatched up the girl and swung her into the saddle.

The only fact in Adah's fable was her presence in Texas. She married Alexander Isaac Menken in Livingston in 1856. Menken, a musician and orchestra leader, was the son of a prominent Jewish family in Cincinnati, and acted as Adah's business manager.

It seems he also figured the latter was a short-term gig, and they'd soon settle down and get on with raising a family. Adah's debut in New York the following year began to divest him of that notion. Although she had no track record as an actress, theater manager James Charles hired her to star in *The Lady of Lyons* and later, *Fazio*.

Talented or not, Adah bedazzled audiences and reviewers alike. She promptly dumped Menken and in 1859, married John Carmel Heenan, otherwise known as Benecia Boy, a barefisted heavyweight boxing champion.

"He attracted me physically," she later said. "In much the same fashion . . . Mark Antony's ardent embraces stirred the tiger-blood in Cleopatra."

A woman admitting to carnal thoughts, much less doing the deed, was a shock (and a turn-on) to Victorians. Her licentiousness and neglect to divorce Menken before marrying her pugilist sparked a national scandal.

Adah may not have originated the concept that bad publicity is better than none at all, but she certainly capitalized on it. Scathing editorials kept her name in the newspapers and zinging from lips to ears all over the country. In response to bigamy charges, she demurely espoused that she "assumed it was the duty of the man of the family to attend to legal matters, including such details as divorce." Which, being a gentleman, Menken did, posthaste.

In 1861, Adah gave birth to Heenan's son, but the baby died in infancy—a heartbreaking loss for his adoring mother. On the wind were allegations that Benecia Boy not only taught his wife to box, but that he often used her as a punching bag. It's doubtful, however, that Adah would take any form of abuse for a second, and the tragedian and publicity hound in her would have portrayed Heenan as Ivan the Terrible's meaner kid brother.

Truth be known, it's a wonder she didn't.

Fate delivered a knockout blow to the marriage and Heenan's championship bout in England with British boxer Tom Sayer. Whether he or Adah executed divorce proceedings, the couple received an official legal divorce.

That same year, she was arrested for carrying a Confederate flag onstage and married husband number three, Robert Henry Newell. The political satirist, pen-named Orpheus C. Kerr (phonetically, "office seeker") was already marital history when Adah was offered the lead in a play titled *Mazeppa, or the Wild Horse of Tartary*.

The production, based on a Lord Byron poem, called for a Tartar prince, who was stripped by his enemies, lashed to a wild horse, and carried off to the mountains to die. Alterations in the script had Adah playing the basic virginal damsel in distress at the mercy of a villain. In the final act, he'd tie her to a horse and utter the dastardly and immortal words, "Now, let the scorching suns and piercing blazes...rend the vile Tartar piecemeal . . ."

Actually, what that vile Tartar, clad in a thin, flesh-colored bodysuit, rended was a mesmerizing effect on a predominantly made audience. No notice whatsoever was taken of her acting ability or the lack thereof. Or that the mountain ledges Adah traversed on her final ride consisted of an elevated ramp disguised by jagged, painted cardboard props.

On opening night, New York theatergoers must have fanned

themselves so frantically, they all but levitated above their seats. Some critics disparaged the play as a circus performance, but the *New York Tribune* reported, "Miss Menken's success on the stage has been attributed to her fine figure, easy carriage and thoroughly debonair deportment."

Professionally, that success mushroomed during The Menken's European tour. Then, even as now, outcries littered with words like *lewd, indecent,* and *nudity* drew crowds.

On the personal front and in no discernible order, Adah married and divorced a gambler named James Barclay, bore and buried another infant son, and became the mistress of Alexandre Dumas. Other literati entranced by her poetry, charm, or both, albeit platonically (probably) were Charles Dickens, Dante Gabriel Rossetti, Algernon Swinburne, and George Sand, who was godmother to the second baby Adah lost.

Returning to the States lengthened the roster of admirers. A Confederate flag draped across her San Francisco hotel room's wall didn't endear her to Union loyalists, but the St. Francis Hook and Ladder Company presented her with a gorgeous fire belt to commemorate induction as an honorary brigade member.

Declaring yellow to be her mystical color, she sashayed about town, a vision of saffron loveliness from head to toe. Joaquin Miller, famed poet and ardent admirer, said, "I doubt if any other woman in the world could wear a dress like that in the winds of San Francisco and not look ridiculous."

Nor, one perceives, could anyone other than The Menken not have sounded ridiculous when, on a horseback ride with Miller in the California desert, she dismounted, prostrated herself, and proclaimed, "I was born in this yellow sand sometime and somewhere . . . in the deserts of Africa, maybe."

In 1864, according to passages in Clair Haffaker's *Profiles of the American West*, Mark Twain, a reporter for the Virginia City, Nevada, *Territorial Enterprise* went frog-eyed at a one-hundred-foot-long poster stretched across the nearby mountain slopes. THE GREAT MAZEPPA writ large crowned a larger, colorful illustration of a woman strapped to a galloping horse like a horizontal Lady Godiva.

The newspaperman would not in his famously wild imaginings ever guess the actress splayed atop that fiery steed's back was fluent in several languages and a published writer. What Mark Twain did supposedly think was that it was his duty as a member of the Fourth Estate to "give that girl her comeuppance. After all, put her clothes back on, and what have you got?"

A singular opinion, as "within an hour," Huffaker wrote, "the most fabulous boomtown of its time was filled with the magic name. Work around the site of the Comstock lode came to a halt." And in the ensuing melee to celebrate her imminent arrival, "two men were shot on 'C' Street and a drunken Chinaman was knifed in McGuire's bar."

An acquaintance of Twain's noted that the equestrienne flirted with death at each performance. One slip, one weak spot in the rickety scenery, and she could be killed. Twain scoffed, certain that when his future review of the melodrama hit print, "she'll just keep riding that mustang clear back to New York."

If Menken were prone to turn tail and run, she'd already be midway across Colorado Territory. A Carson City *Independent* writer had written of Mazeppa's leading lady:

> We hope there were no butchers in the audience, for they must have been lost to the play, and thought of nothing but veal.

Such Calves! they were never reared on milk. The acting consisted of sneezing, smoking, and coughing on the part of the supes, and some elegant posturing on the part of The Menken.

Twain attended the Virginia City performance with the balance of the *Enterprise*'s editorial staff, Dan DeQuille (William Wright) and publisher, Joe Goodman. Also in the audience was gambler Nat Redding, who popped a seven-thousand-dollar diamond-studded jacket button when, exclusively for that night's finale (according to one account), the villain's henchmen stripped Adah bare to the waist.

When the *Enterprise* staff returned to the newspaper office to compose their reviews, DeQuille allegedly asked Mark Twain, "What are you going to find fault with?" A still-perspiring Twain replied, "I'm going to find fault with the English language. It hasn't got the words to describe such a magnificent creature as The Menken."

Evidently he and the others dredged up enough to make the rest of the cast feel invisible. Their verbal sour grapes induced Adah to halt the next night's performance in the third act and "demand that everyone in this company apologize to Mr. Twain and Mr. DeQuille."

During her extended stay, she became the mistress of Tom Peasley, a wealthy miner and cohort of Twain and DeQuille. Overnight, a street and a new mine were named for her. A group of prospectors presented her with a solid bar of silver assayed at two thousand dollars. Not to be outdone, partners in another new diggings christened it The Menken Shaft and Tunnel Company and gave Adah fifty shares of stock worth five thousand dollars. (She later sold them for a thousand dollars each.)

Any hearts yet unwon by the visiting goddess were surrendered one night in the Sazerac saloon after she boasted that thanks to her second husband's private lessons, she could outbox any man in the place.

The first contender went down in the first round. A smart uppercut dropped the second man to one knee. Egged on by catcalls, he forgot all those youthful teachings about hitting girls. He struck back with three consecutive roundhouses that Adah ducked and danced away from with ease . . . then felled him with a solid right to the jaw.

No sooner had Adah vowed she'd live out her days in Virginia City than the inevitable happened: her horse stumbled up the ramp. She loosed the rope instantly and was only grazed as the animal slammed to the stage, but she and the entire audience were shaken by the accident.

A month later, Tom Peasley found her hotel room empty. She'd decamped in the middle of the night, without a word or a note to anyone. Peasley was devastated.

Some historians speculate that the hoof-cut she sustained in the accident wasn't healing. It either aroused suspicions or confirmed rumors that she was slowly dying of tuberculosis.

Mazeppa's second European tour didn't rate the rave reviews the first had. Twice more, her horse lost its footing. One spill broke her hand and wrist; in the second, a flailing hoof lacerated the skin a fraction below her throat. Increasingly fatigued, feeling her life slipping away, she finished a book of poetry titled *Infelicia*, dedicated to Charles Dickens and edited by Algernon Swinburne's secretary.

The following is a segment of "Drifts That Bar My Door." Maudlin it might be, yet no more so than others of her era:

Life is a lie, and Love a cheat.
There is a graveyard in my poor heart—dark, heaped-up
graves, from which no flowers spring.
The walls are so high, that the trembling wings of birds do
not break ere they reach the summit, and then fall,
wounded, and die in my bosom.
I wander 'mid the gray old tombs, and talk with the ghosts of
my buried hopes.
They tell me of my Eros, and how they fluttered around him,
bearing sweet messages of my love, until one day, with his
strong arm, he struck them dead at his feet.

The Menken died in Paris on August 10, 1868, of tuberculosis complicated by acute peritonitis. She was buried in Montparnasse cemetery, and at her request, her tomb was engraved, THOU KNOWEST.

The brief eulogy that appeared in a Parisian newspaper read

Ungrateful animals, mankind;
Walking his rider's hearse behind,
Mourner-in-chief her horse appears,
But where are all her cavaliers?

One of them, it seems, was busy taking a posthumous potshot at a supposedly beloved friend. Of Adah's poetry book, published eight days after she died, Charles Dickens sneered, "She is a sensitive poet who, unfortunately, cannot write."

A century after her death, an episode of the popular television series *Bonanza* was titled "The Magnificent Adah." Ruth Roman played the part of The Menken, whom the Cartwright brothers believed was angling to become the next Mrs. Ben Cartwright.

The Grave of Ann Rutledge, Petersburg, Illinois (Library of Congress, LC-USZ62-133038)

12

WILMA FRANCES MINOR
CLARA DeBOYER
ANN RUTLEDGE

I would die on the gallows that the spirits of
Ann and Abe were speaking through my Mother to me . . .

An enigma, it seems, is fair game for idle, if not rampant and endless, speculation. There's just something about a brooding, sphinxlike demeanor that implies a dark, deep-rooted cause.

Abraham Lincoln, for instance. Almost a century and a half after his assassination, scholars and scientists debate whether his dour physiognomy was symptomatic of Marfan syndrome, manic depression, migraines, acute presbyopia, transient apnea, petit mal seizures, and heaven knows what else.

It stands to reason that photographs and portraits of the

Civil War president would reflect the inner turmoil plaguing a divided nation's commander-in-chief. Yet, absent his trademark facial hair, a circa 1845 daguerreotype portrays the same introspective Lincoln, his gray eyes set in cavernous sockets, staring into bleak oblivion.

The tall, spindly, backwoods Illinois lawyer who became the sixteenth president never cut a dashing figure, but one would think a popular congressman and father of four would appear a tad happier about life in general and his own, specifically. And if not, why not?

Because of a heart permanently broken at age twenty-six by the death of Ann Rutledge, the love of his life, proclaimed Wilma Frances Minor, a part-time reporter and columnist for the San Diego *Union*.

In her 1928 letter addressed to Edward A. Meeks, of the Atlantic Monthly Press, Wilma said, "I have just finished writing the 'true love story' of Abraham Lincoln and Ann Rutledge," based on family papers and original letters from Lincoln to his beloved Ann, that Wilma had inherited.

Harper's, she went on, ". . . have been very anxious to get it," but if her book was eligible for the Press's five-thousand-dollar biennial award, she knew ". . . a prize book gets such wide acclaim and the material is worthy of the best."

Edward Meeks showed Wilma Minor's letter to *Atlantic Monthly* owner and editor Ellery Sedgwick. Ivy League educated, wed to a Cabot, hence the epitome of a crusty New Englander, Sedgwick perused the letter, then followed his own oft-given advice: ". . . In any encounter with improbability, he [an editor] should put on the brakes gently but let the motor run."

His motor revved up a notch upon receipt of Wilma Minor's typed, 227-page manuscript and photostatic copies of the Lincoln letters. It shifted into overdrive when he met the enchanting, hazel-eyed authoress in person.

By contrast, her mother and traveling companion, Clara De-Boyer, was described by Edward Meeks as "tall and beady-eyed, with hair suspiciously black for her age" that conjured images of a fortune-teller.

Ellery Sedgwick was neither blind to Wilma's bodacious figure, nor immune to her bounteous charm, but for a magazine editor, her most desirable asset was evidence confirming the enduring rumors about Lincoln's and Rutledge's ill-fated romance.

Abe most assuredly did meet Ann in the 1830s in New Salem, Illinois. He boarded at the tavern her family owned, earning his keep variously as a rail-splitter, surveyor, grocery clerk, and the village postmaster. At the time, the Rutledges' bright, fetching nineteen-year-old daughter was engaged to John McNamar (or McNeil), except Ann suspected John's excuses for delaying his return from a trip to New York were a jilting-in-progress.

At some point, according to local legend, Abe and Ann fell madly in love. They planned to marry, but Ann insisted on waiting until she could ask McNamar "for formal renunciation of his claim on her."

Alas, by the summer of 1835, Ann's health was in obvious decline. She died of brain fever (meningitis) on August 25, 1835, allegedly a loss from which a grief-stricken future president would never recover.

Wilma Minor wasn't the first to present evidence confirming the rumor. In November 1866, less than two years after President Lincoln was laid to rest, William H. Herndon, his friend and longtime law partner, presented a series of lectures asserting Lincoln's eternal love for Ann.

The Shadows Rise, by John Evangelist Walsh, notes that Herndon's lectures were of three hours' duration, during which, he stated, "The facts . . . making a complete history, lie in fragments in the desk at my office, in the bureau drawers at my home, and in my memory . . ."

Over the years, numerous Lincoln biographers either dismissed the romance as bunk, ignored it entirely, or repeated it as probable but unproved. Ida Tarbell's works on Lincoln dating back to the 1890s took the latter tack, whereas Carl Sandburg's *Abraham Lincoln: The Prairie Years*, published in 1926, demonstrates its poet-author's love for the love story.

Contributing heavily to the legend-as-fact was the Edgar Lee Masters poem graven on Ann Rutledge's headstone in Oakland Cemetery, Petersburg, Illinois:

Out of me unworthy and unknown
The vibrations of deathless music!
"With malice toward none, with charity for all."
Out of me the forgiveness of millions toward millions,
And the beneficent face of a nation
Shining with justice and truth.
I am ANN RUTLEDGE who sleep beneath these weeds,
Beloved of ABRAHAM LINCOLN,
Wedded to him, not through union,
But through separation.
Bloom forever, O Republic,
From the dust of my bosom!

Detracting equally as heavily from this stone-chiseled epitaph is the fact that Ann's coffin was moved from the Concord, Illinois, cemetery to Oakland in 1890 and the poetic headstone not set until 1921.

Strangely enough, Edgar Lee Masters's book, *Lincoln—The Man*, published in 1931, stated that ". . . Lincoln had no lasting love, if any love, for Ann Rutledge" and the story was naught but William H. Herndon's fond delusion.

The prospect of putting to rest sixty-odd years of controversy made Ellery Sedgwick's pulse race. To capitalize on Wilma Minor's "Lincoln the Lover" story, it was slated as a three-part series, starting with *Atlantic Monthly's* December 1928 issue—the circulation-boosting answer to an editor's prayer. Later, the material would be expanded to book length and published by the Press.

The deal struck with Miss Minor netted her fifteen hundred dollars for the serialization, a thousand-dollar advance on the book, and an additional four thousand on publication. While $6,500 may not sound like a windfall by modern standards, in 1928, beef was six cents a pound, movie tickets cost a quarter, and a spanking-new Studebaker Erskine Six complete with rumble seat sold for $985.

The rush to print left Sedgwick scant time for authenticating Wilma's packet of Lincoln letters, but he tried. Sort of.

The photostats underwent a brief examination when Reverend William E. Barton, a "bloodhound after the facts" regarding Lincoln, dropped by Sedgwick's office. Barton knew Lincoln's signature was forged more often than any historical figure's and wasn't about to stamp approval on blurred copies of the originals. He did, however, remark that the collection seemed rather too good to be true.

Undaunted, Sedgwick sent a batch of photostats to Worthington Chauncey Ford, editor of the Massachusetts Historical Society, who'd completed the deceased Albert J. Beveridge's biography of Lincoln.

Not until September 21 did one of several parcels containing the original letters and documentation from Wilma Minor land on Sedgwick's desk. All told, the packets included books bearing Lincoln's signature and margin notes, diary pages written by Matilda Cameron, Ann Rutledge's cousin, and reams of letters by Wilma's forebears that scribed a family tree branching from Rutledge to Frederick Hirth, Wilma's greatuncle.

In the meantime, Worthington Ford declared the photostats in no way resembled Lincoln's handwriting. Dr. Barton, who'd also expressed reservations about the photostats, had repaired to Vanderbilt University, where he was a faculty member.

Eyes riveted on the calendar, Sedgwick deleted both Ford and Barton from the list to receive samples of the originals. Instead, he sent them to Ida N. Tarbell, Carl Sandburg, and a commercial chemist for an analysis of the paper and ink.

Sedgwick's assistant, Theodore Morrison, was assigned the task of conforming Wilma Minor's hideously purple prose ("Night, like a black, sinewy panther, crawled cautiously through the unbending straight directness of the saplings on the river bank.") to *Atlantic* standards.

The issue's frontispiece was also being drafted. The final read, in part:

This chapter out of the life of Lincoln has always been shrouded in mystery . . . Imagine then, our incredulity when the Wilma Frances Minor collection first appeared, our amazement that authentic Lincoln letters had defied the most diligent research of the biographer, and our delight when the material passed test after test put to it by the country's most distinguished Lincoln scholars.

In San Diego, Miss Minor, who'd been quoted as saying she'd "read fairy tales and believed them long past the age of most children," felt like Cinderella at the ball. Speaking invitations poured in. The San Diego chapter of the League of American Penwomen welcomed Wilma into their august fold. Rare document collectors, dealers, and auction houses declared the letters priceless, then asked her to name hers. There was talk of adapting "Lincoln the Lover" for film, or the stage.

In Boston, Ellery Sedgwick was receiving his share of excellent news. Ida N. Tarbell wrote, "My faith is strong that you have an amazing set of true Lincoln documents—the most extraordinary that have come to us in many years." The other short-notice expert, Carl Sandburg opined, "These new Lincoln letters seem entirely authentic—and preciously and wonderfully co-ordinate and chime with all else known of Lincoln." As a bonus, the chemist confirmed the composition of the letters' paper and ink were consistent with early nineteenth-century writing materials.

The December 1928 issue of the *Atlantic Monthly* with Wilma Minor's debut installment of "Lincoln the Lover" was an unqualified barn-burner. Trouble was, the heat it generated wasn't the type Ellery Sedgwick envisioned.

Worthington Ford fired the first salvo. He railed at Sedgwick, "Have you gone insane or have I?" and accused the editor of "putting over one of the crudest forgeries I have known." Paul M. Angle, secretary of the Lincoln Centennial Society in Springfield, Illinois, concurred: "One doesn't get a chance very often to put the magazine of the country into the frying pan and cook it brown."

Carl Sandburg defended the letters' authenticity in print on December 4, only to acknowledge the next day that the documents were probably fake. Ida Tarbell straddled the fence somewhat by saying, "When I scrutinize original source material of this kind I let my emotions have full play. I try to do my hard-boiled analyzing later."

Leading Lincoln experts whose opinions Sedgwick had either ignored or failed to solicit joined forces and pored over an advance copy of the second installment. Among the discrepancies: Some letters were signed *Abe*, a nickname Lincoln detested and never used. Matilda Cameron never existed, hence pages from her "diary" were totally fabricated. Ann Rutledge's purported writings mentioned Spencer's copybook, which wasn't published until thirteen years after her death. A Lincoln missive referred to a family leaving for "someplace in Kansas," two decades before Kansas acquired its name and the region was open for settlement.

Not coincidentally, Minor's deceased great-uncle, Frederick Hirth, the supposed source of all the materials, had resided in Emporia, Kansas.

Sedgwick's letter to Wilma Minor, admitting that the negative outcry was mounting and damning, earned her blithe telegraph: "Situation gives no cause for alarm."

Wilma's optimism didn't deter the magazine's business manager from hiring a Los Angeles detective agency to investigate her background. The circulation manager, Teresa Fitzpatrick, consulted a handwriting expert.

Before either report was received, Wilma's mother, Clara DeBoyer's personal note to Fitzpatrick unwittingly blew off the proverbial lid: DeBoyer's handwriting was identical to that in the Lincoln letters.

When confronted, DeBoyer and Minor denied the forgery. Wilma claimed they'd been deceived by Scott Greene, the son of one of Lincoln's friends in New Salem, whom Minor interviewed a year earlier for a San Diego *Union* profile.

Although Ellery Sedgwick had promised an exposé of the fraud the two women had perpetrated, he announced at a staff meeting in May 1929 that the magazine's lawyers had advised against it.

Teresa Fitzpatrick wasn't content to let the matter drop. In July, she went to San Diego and met with Wilma Minor and Clara DeBoyer. As it turned out, Edward Meek's initial impression of Mrs. DeBoyer's resemblance to a fortune-teller was eerily on target. And the true story (tru*er*, anyway) was more bizarre than the fiction they'd sold as fact to Ellery Sedgwick.

According to Wilma, she was inspired by her newspaper interview with Scott Greene to ask her mother to use her "second sight" to channel a spirit guide. Wilma's role in the séance would be "the instrument through whom the real story might come to the world."

Through DeBoyer, the spirit guide said he'd get back to Wilma next week. When netherworldly approval of the arrangement was granted, a number of spiritual conference calls ensued. Wilma wrote out questions. DeBoyer channeled them to various guides, from Rutledge and Lincoln to Rutledge's cousin, Matilda Cameron (who never existed in this world, but somehow teleported to the next), to deceased family members. Whatever the guide answered, DeBoyer transcribed, as though taking dictation.

A guide even directed Wilma to go forth and buy books of the correct vintage and use the blank sheets as writing paper. How and where the nigh century-old ink was obtained wasn't clarified.

If a hoax had been perpetrated, which Wilma and Clara adamantly denied, those wily spirit guides were the guilty parties. All mother and daughter did was give them "voice."

As far as known, the pair avoided prosecution. It's presumed Ellery Sedgwick and *Atlantic Monthly* had suffered enough without initiating a civil lawsuit. And criminal charges would be difficult to prosecute without Sedgwick's cooperation.

The enduring question remains: Was Abraham Lincoln's chronic melancholia caused by the death of Ann Rutledge? Because no one on this astral plane can say for certain, the controversy may never be laid to rest.

(Library of Congress, LC-USZ62-113383)

13

ELISABET NEY

Even to sit at a table where human beings are
devouring the flesh of dead animals is for me most nauseating.

Quite a statement, considering the general time period
(1890s), the locale being Austin, Texas, the then beef-
on-the-hoof capital of the world and that Elisabet was a dinner guest of that city's premiere social maven and widow of a
former governor, Sarah Pease.

In modern vernacular, Elisabet didn't quite fit the phrase, "a
one-owner." Her quirks defied generalization, but it's nearer the
peg than copiously watered-down depictions such as, "the great
German individualist."

Franzisca Bernardina Wilhelmina Elizabet Ney was born in
Munster, Westphalia, Germany, on January 26, 1833. She was the
second surviving child and only daughter of hausfrau Anna
Elizabet and Johann Adam Ney, a skilled stonecutter of statuary
and gravestones. Johann proudly and often spoke of his sup-

posed uncle, legendary Field Marshal Michel Ney, Napoléon's close friend and most admired general.

The Neys were upper middle-class German Catholics who spoiled their headstrong daughter simply by failing to discipline her. By no means a sugar-and-spice, doll-playing, lace-and-ruffle little girl, Elisabet fought constantly with her older brother, Fritz, and ignored her mother, who received scant if any backup in the behavior department from Elisabet's father.

One doesn't think of the nineteenth century as a mother–daughter battleground over wardrobe, but at the age of ten, Elisabet flatly refused to wear the *de rigueur* frilly embroidered dresses, and so she designed her own clothes: Grecian-style, flowing robes inspired by the angels and saint figures her father chiseled in his workshop.

St. Martin's School for Girls didn't temper Elisabet's temperament, or assumably, her bizarre outfits. Having spent years watching Johann craft beautiful seraphim from blocks of stone, mimicking his technique and adapting her own, she declared she'd never marry (a form of slavery, she proclaimed) and never become a deferential, shriveled old hausfrau like her mother.

It was Elisabet's dream and her "destiny" to attend the Academy of Art in Berlin. She would become the world's greatest living female sculptor, so it followed she must study under Christian Daniel Rauch, at that time Germany's greatest living sculptor.

Elisabet was gifted, but even if her father could afford the tuition, the Academy didn't accept female students. Elisabet's response was a hunger strike, as though starvation was the answer to cash-flow problems and discrimination.

With the bishop's assistance, a compromise was reached, whereby Elisabet would attend the art school in Munich. She agreed, believing two years' training there would magically enlarge the family bank account and open the Academy's door.

Her extraordinary talent accomplished the latter, although the Academy's first female student was accepted on a four-month trial basis. If in any way she proved to be a distraction, gifted or not, she'd be expelled. As for the tuition her parents refused to pay, fearing Berlin's hotbed of nonconformity would unduly influence their daughter, Elisabet was prepared to suffer for her art.

Not that she missed any meals, let alone got a job to finance her advanced studies. She fell in love with a medical student named Edmund Duncan Montgomery—an avant-garde philosopher with a trust fund—and Edmund chivalrously sponsored her education. The illegitimate son of a Scottish baron and his strangely rigid eccentric lover, Edmund wanted to marry the tall, berobed, curly-mopped redhead. He wrote decades later of their relationship, "We pledged ourselves in our student days in Munich to live an ideal life together," meaning free of possessiveness—legal or emotional.

Christian Rauch was enchanted by his protégée, even providing her studio space. According to two of Ney's biographers, Jan Fortune and Jean Burton, "like Rauch, 'she combined ideal conception with masterly technical execution,'" and some critics claimed, "she already surpassed her teacher."

Her fame and social popularity were flourishing, not in small part due to Edmund Montgomery's contacts and her success at another aim: rubbing elbows with the famous and powerful. The head she sculpted of master violinist Joseph Joachim was among her best-known and admired early works, along with sculptures of King George V, scientist Alexander von Humboldt, and the only bust ever made of Bismarck, Chancellor of Germany.

The bust she created of George V's court painter, Friedrich Kaulbach, in return for the portrait Kaulbach painted of her, touched off rumors of a love affair. It was not the first time Elisabet was linked with someone other than Edmund Montgomery. The possibility of her roving eye presented a quandary for a man dedicated to the pursuit of free, unpossessive, nonavaricious love, although one of Elizabet's friends reportedly observed, "Seldom has a German woman had so many admirers—or cared so little about them."

Elisabet's commission from Queen Victoria for a marble sculpture effected a turning point in her relationship with Edmund. Learning her beau was on the island of Madiera and seriously, if not mortally, stricken with tuberculosis, Elisabet rushed to his side. Accounts of what transpired vary (Edmund begging her to be his wife, or issuing an ultimatum), but the couple was married on November 17, 1863.

Within days, Elisabet stormed off alone to Formosa, the honeymoon villa Edmund had built for her. Could be she believed the ceremony a "mercy marriage," thus an understandable, compassionate, and temporary modification of her vow never to marry. Or cold feet didn't strike until after the deed was done.

Whatever the circumstances, to the amusement and irritation of the neighbors, after several days' loud arguments between Elisabet on Formosa's balcony and a locked-out Edmund on the street below, she exacted his promise they'd never, ever admit to anyone that they were holy wedlocked. She'd refer to him as her best friend, and he'd introduce her as Miss Ney.

Edmund's mother, who was considerably less than impressed with her daughter-in-law (that sculptor-woman can't boil an egg), gave over her maid, Crescentia (Cencie), lest the poor, recovering consumptive die of neglect.

An evidently unexpected glitch in Elisabet's unrecognized marriage occurred in December 1870, when to her horror, she discovered she was pregnant. Because she preferred to emigrate to the United States and found a Utopian community in Georgia to admitting she and Edmund were legally wed, the Scotsman, his pregnant German non-wife, and German maid settled in swampy, mosquito-infested Thomasville, Georgia.

There, Elisabet gave birth to Arthur Montgomery, whom she glibly and forever referred to as her "bastard son." As for the progressive community they hoped to establish in Reconstructionist Georgia, it was doomed from the start. The women didn't speak English. Cencie contracted malaria. All three were pathetic farmers, and townspeople regarded them as foreign abolitionist carpetbaggers.

Obsessed with finding a sanctuary with a climate similar to Italy's, they roamed from Maine to Guatemala, stopping long enough in Red Wing, Minnesota, for Elisabet to bear her other quasi-illegitimate son, Lorne.

Ever the romanticist in art, life, and love, in March 1873,

Elisabet took one look at Liendo, a 1,100-acre plantation in Waller County, Texas, and proclaimed, "Here will I live and here will I die."

The sixteen-room, two-story Georgian house and property was what contemporary Realtors would deem a fixer-upper, if not a white elephant. The Civil War had not treated the mansion or grounds kindly. The property had changed hands several times since—primarily due to the number of servants and fieldhands necessary to work the place.

Its isolation wasn't an amenity to anyone but Edmund and Elisabet. Nor was five miles-distant Hempstead's nicknames: The Hell Hole of Texas, and Six-Shooter Junction.

Edmund set up a library-study-laboratory in the house to research and produce such esoterically titled papers as "To Be Alive—What Is It?"

By day Cencia managed the house. At night, she slept on a cot in front of Elisabet's locked bedroom door—almost certainly, a form of birth control.

Elisabet oversaw the farmworkers—on horseback, forking the saddle (not riding sidesaddle), and attired in purple satin bloomers or Grecian robes cinched by a brace of pistols and a black velvet cape furling behind her.

Suffice it to say, for a cotton farmer, she was a great German sculptor. Her getups and imperious manner at once humored and raised her employees' hackles, as well as the Hempsteadians, all of whom she referred to as "peasants."

Her nigh-boastful remarks regarding her sons' illegitimacy, comparisons of marriage to slavery, and polemic disparagements of organized religion didn't endear her to the natives. Why, those hardscrabble pioneers even remained unanimously unimpressed by the necklace given Elisabet by the King of Prussia, a diamond-and-emerald bracelet from George V and Queen Victoria, and a breast-watch from Ludwig of Bavaria.

By summer, any remaining molecule of goodwill toward Elisabet evaporated with the death of her two-year-old son, Arthur. The tragedy and its aftermath have been glossed over by many biographers, or the cause of the child's death attributed to diphtheria. Which may be true, except a single case of diphtheria—an extremely contagious disease—is virtually unheard of, and there are no references to anyone else at Liendo becoming ill—eight-month-old Lorne, in particular.

Another curiosity is a few mentions of Edmund's frantic search of his medical books in an attempt to diagnose and treat his son. It appears he was never certified as a doctor, but did train for years at several universities, thus should have recognized diphtheria's telltale symptoms: high fever; white lesions on the gums, lips, tonsils, and throat; swollen, sensitive glands; an angled jaw; hemorrhaging at the nostrils and mouth.

Whatever the two-year-old died of, Elisabet carried his lifeless body upstairs to her room and bolted the door, where she allegedly spent all night crafting a death mask of her son and a sculpture of his body.

The next morning, after Edmund kicked in the door, she carried Arthur downstairs and ordered Cencie to stack a fireplace with kindling. Elisabet poured oil over her son's body, knelt on the hearth, and struck a match. Hours later, she filled a leather shot pouch with the cooled ashes, locked the door to the room, and never entered it again.

Whatever the boy succumbed to, it was not neglect, abuse, or murder. Elisabet wasn't thrilled at becoming a mother, but she often called Arthur "beautiful" and "perfect." Her posthumous sculpture seems bizarre, unless one thinks of it as a mother employing her artistic gift to create a lasting memorial to her firstborn child—different, yet similar to the practice of preserving strands of a deceased loved one's hair for watch fobs, or a piece of jewelry.

Edmund may have cited diphtheria to horrified employees and townspeople to explain Arthur's cremation as a precaution against an epidemic. After all, those Elisabet had insulted and ridiculed would not have been satisfied with a declared atheist laying her child's death to "God's will."

Edmund's and Elisabet's grief was profound. For the most part, solace wasn't taken from or given to each other. Edmund retreated to his study, devoting himself to microscopically examining protoplasm, "the visible, tangible manifestation of all vitality."

Elisabet's short, auburn curls faded to white. Working to exhaustion, trying to eke a profit from Liendo's soil, left no time to sculpt. Outwardly, she remained the Grecian-gowned foreigner adrift with royal jewelry and in hock up to her eyeballs. Inwardly, the artist was dying by inches.

In 1879, Governor Oran Milo Roberts contacted the only sculptor in Texas about creating life-size sculptures of Sam Houston and Stephen F. Austin for the new white limestone capitol building in Austin. Elisabet was ecstatic. She remained so, even after some quick political string-pulling got the building material changed to Llano red granite and statues stricken from the budget.

Fingers gripping the tools of her art for the first time in a decade, she warmed up with a bust of herself, then Edmund, then from photographs, one of President James Garfield. All, alas, for naught. The Garfield work received some attention, but no commissions. Again, she put away her chisels and focused on a living model for her next project: her eleven-year-old son, Lorne.

The boy had grown up on tales of the Napoleonic Ney's derring-do and nobility, his European and Scottish birthright, his future place mingling with royals and their retinues. Elisabet already dressed the boy, whose hair curled to his shoulders, in velvet suits. Nicknamed Little Lord Fauntleroy (and worse), Lorne was homeschooled by foreign-born tutors, but ventures from Liendo resulted in black eyes, bruises, and skinned knuckles.

Lorne fought back and gave as good as he got, but the new wardrobe his mother fashioned for him was the final straw. "Nightshirt! Nightshirt!" the townies catcalled when Lorne appeared in a Grecian robe.

Adolescence brings rebellion, and arguably, Lorne had more reasons to lash out than did others his age. Elisabet did sculpt a stunning bust of him, which she titled *The Head of a Young Violinist*, as though homage to her old friend Joseph Joachim ordained a self-fulfilling prophesy in her son.

Like a horse trainer who believes beating an animal into submission is the best way to tame it, Elisabet railed at Lorne for willfully neglecting his heritage. She spewed vicious denials that he was her son—that she'd never had any children and had found him abandoned in a fisherman's hut.

Lorne fired back, deriding his mother's art—her Achilles'

heel. Over the years, they coexisted but never reconciled. The wounds were too deep, and both mother and son, too stubborn and proud to forgive.

Oran Roberts finally came through with a commission for Elisabet: statues of Sam Houston, Stephen F. Austin, and Albert Sidney Johnston for the Texas exhibit at the Chicago World's Fair. The catch was that although materials and a studio in Austin the capitol's basement would be provided, the job didn't pay a dime.

Liendo was mortgaged to the hilt. It had gobbled the inheritances Elisabet and Edmund received from their respective parents. Elisabet had posted a notice in the Hempstead newspaper: *To my creditors: Please don't bother to send me any bills. I have no money.*

And couldn't care less, now that she'd secured her first commission in America. The plaster led to dividing her time between Liendo and Austin, where she later designed a studio dubbed Formosa for the long-ago honeymoon villa that wasn't.

While her half-castle, half-Grecian-studio was under construction, Elisabet camped nearby in a tent awash with Oriental shawls, tapestries, and rugs. When the studio was finished, she strung a hammock to sleep in under the portico, accessible by a ladder, although her youth and figure were now mere memories. Edmund's sleeping quarters during visits to Elisabet's home away from home was a tent on the lawn—either by choice or by command.

It was at Formosa that she recreated Stephen F. Austin and Sam Houston in marble, along with what could be termed her

Confederate series: pioneer Texas Ranger General W. P. Harde-
man, Jefferson Davis, and General Joe Johnston.

Visitors—invited or not—never knew whether they'd be
welcomed or ignored. Those whom she received and served tea
and toast, or clabber (thickened, curdled milk) included
Pavlova, Enrico Caruso, Sarah Pease, and an adoring cadre of
art students.

It's said Austinites timed their carriage rides around a pond
adjacent to Formosa (Elisabet called it a lake) with her parasol-
shaded cruises across the water in a canoe fitted with pillows.
Rather than hire a Negro manservant, as was customary, Elisabet employed an Indian named Horace, whose duties extended
to paddling her about like a portly, seventy-something Cleopatra on her barge.

A sight it was, to be sure, but what the spectators hoped to
witness was one of Elisabet's frequent hissies in regard to Horace's paddling. At such times, she'd either wrest the oar from
him for a demonstration or stand up to give him what-for,
tump over the whole shebang, and then wade ashore, scowling
and drenched to the skin.

It was at Formosa that she sculpted her masterpiece, Lady
Macbeth, posed as though sleepwalking after murdering King
Duncan. Elisabet said her creation was so beautiful, she "can't
bear to look at it more than a few minutes." Not out of egotism,
but from a pure sense of wonder only a true artist possesses and
can understand.

In May 1907, Elisabet suffered a stroke and was cared for by
the Sisters of the Holy Cross. The faithful and in many ways
long-suffering Edmund was with her when she suffered a fatal

heart attack on June 29. What is described as akin to a state funeral was held in Austin. An editor's eulogy, reproduced in *The Women*, declared,

> An account of the present state of art in Texas is chiefly an account of our great sculptor, Elisabet Ney. It is needless to ask by what unexpected beneficence of fortune an artist, who was the glory of the most cultured art center of Europe, was vouchsafed to an obscure young State. God loves Texas; let that suffice to explain so delightful a miracle.

Elisabet Ney was buried in a copse of live oaks she and Edmund had planted thirty years earlier. Lorne, now twice married and the father of five, Cencie, Edmund, and the two Negroes who dug the grave were the only attendants.

Four years later, Edmund joined the woman who never acknowledged him as her husband in that shady, peaceful final resting place. According to the Fortune and Burton biography, the ever-loyal Cencie laid a flower and a small basket containing Arthur's ashes in Edmund's coffin. She then burned thousands of pieces of correspondence, papers, and documents, perhaps in keeping with Edmund's or Elisabet's wishes, perhaps of her own accord.

A portion of Elisabet's sculpture was donated to the University of Texas; another went to Southern Methodist University. Much of it, her tools and memorabilia, were donated to the Elisabet Ney Museum, formerly known as Formosa—along with Liendo, her favorite place on earth.

Also according to the Fortune and Burton biography, at some unspecified time, looters, hoping to make off with a presumed cache of money or jewels, broke into a leather box Elisabet always kept near her, and that Cencie had overlooked.

Inside was the plaster cast of Arthur, her firstborn son, swaddled in oiled silk.

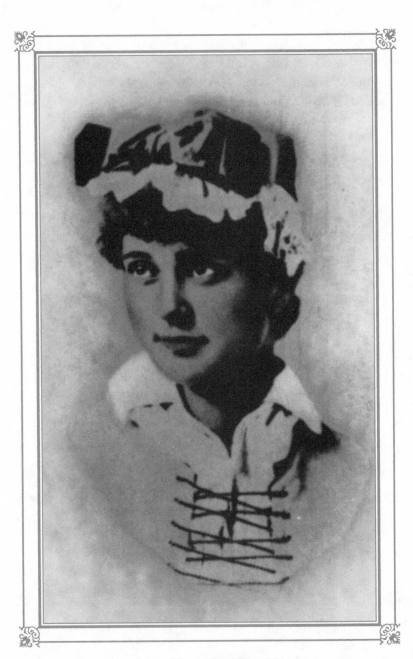

(Library of Congress, LC-USZ62-101367)

14

SARA PARTON
(Fanny Fern)

I never had the slightest intention of writing a book.
Had such a thought entered my mind, I should not have entertained it.
It would have seemed presumptuous.

In an article for Houghton Mifflin's educational division, contributing editor Barbara A. White said, "When I was in graduate school studying nineteenth-century American literature, female writers other than Emily Dickinson were mentioned only to be ridiculed. . . . I don't recall the professors ever referring to . . . 'Fanny Fern.'"

Sara Parton's nom de plume may be frumpy, but the woman who coined the phrase, "The way to a man's heart is through his stomach" is one of the few writers of either gender whose essays transcend a century and a half.

Despite her father's intention to name his fifth-born child

Grata Payson Willis, the baby girl born in Portland, Maine, on July 9, 1811, was christened Sarah Payson Willis. (At some point, she began signing her first name sans the *h*.)

After the family moved to Boston, Deacon Nathaniel Willis and his wife, Hannah, were blessed with four more children, yet the couple was as opposite in personality as two people could be.

Whether Nathaniel was at all happy-go-lucky before his religious conversion to Calvinism, he was a cold, gloomy fish afterward. Sara's mother, Hannah, was dependably cheerful and affectionate toward her brood, but she bore the brunt of her husband's unwarranted castigations. Hannah said not a word in defense, nor ever complained, but Sara resented the tears that rose in her mother's eyes.

Not that Sara's childhood was dismal—the mice, as it were, did play, while Father was away. "The first tragedy of her life," as she later called it, and an example of the irrepressible humor she'd become famous for, is paraphrased in Joyce W. Warren's biography, *Fanny Fern: An Independent Woman*: "One summer when Sara was a very little girl, she broke her doll and was given a crookneck squash to play with. She later described . . . her squash doll was accidentally cooked for dinner and her brother Nat told her that she was a cannibal because she had eaten it."

To her father's dismay and disgust, Sara's tomboyishness and high spirits weren't fazed by his and Calvinist brethren's unending threats of hellfire and brimstone.

She wasn't disrespectful or agnostic. Women's prayer meetings she attended with her mother were peaceful, serene—everything her father's rants were not. Memories of both and other recollections of childhood were reiterated years later in an article titled, "Children's Rights."

A number of wrongs against children were related, including her idea of church, "on the quiet blessed Sabbath, where the minister—like our dear Saviour—sometimes remembered to 'take little children in his arms and bless them.'"

Sara attended a deacon-approved elementary school and later, a series of female seminaries in Massachusetts, for, as she remarked, "algebra and safekeeping." Mathematics wasn't her forte, and Sara was said to be "dangerously inclined to levity." Her satirical compositions would be a prime example of that levity: "Suggestions on Arithmetic," portrayed the tribulations preceding a math exam. "The Child Whom Nobody Can Do Anything With," is self-explanatory.

At twenty, Sara's extensive formal and "useless" education ended, and her mother set to the task of teaching Sara domestic skills. Though a passable-fair sewer, Sara found cooking was fraught with disaster—her habit of stashing novels in her apron pocket and reading them on the sly didn't help. Condemned as "messengers of the devil" and "promoters of obsessive delusions" by religious leaders more liberal than Deacon Willis guaranteed the books an avid, underground readership.

She also continued to proofread the religious tracts and newsletters her father wrote, printed, and distributed and was entrusted with composing fillers—unpaid, on-the-job training for a career Sara would someday pursue in desperation.

On May 4, 1837, she married "Handsome Charley" Harrington Eldredge, an ambitious bank cashier. No sooner had the newlyweds moved in with Charley's parents than it was obvious that his mother, Mary, was the possessive type who'd indulged her only surviving child and wasn't eager to share him with a daughter-in-law.

The younger Eldredges were still in residence a year later, when Sara gave birth to a daughter, Mary. Excerpts from a later essay, titled, "The Invalid Wife" in Warren's biography express Sara's frustration with the childbirth's customary weeks of confinement:

> You are upon a sick bed; a little, feeble thing lies upon your arm, that you might crush with one hand . . . By and by [nurse] comes in,—after staying down[stairs] long enough to get a refreshing cup of coffee,—and walks up to the bed with a bowl of gruel, tasting it, and then putting the spoon back into the bowl. In the first place, you hate gruel; in the next, you couldn't eat it, if she held a pistol to your head, after that spoon has been in her mouth . . . "Dear Charley" . . . gives you a kiss, lights his cigar at the fire, half strangles the new baby with the first whiff, and takes your heart off with him down street! . . . And you lie there and eat that gruel! and pick the fuzz all off the blanket, and make faces at the nurse under the sheet, and wish Eve had never ate that apple.

After they bought their first house in Brighton, near Boston, Charley's parents promptly moved to Brighton, as well. But free to decorate her own house, Sara disliked "the 'unsociable' appearance of rooms which were kept only for company." Home, to her, was "a work-basket here, and a book . . . there, a thumbmark on the door, a few gingerbread crumbs, little worn-out shoes . . ."—all housewifely heresy, and one can imagine her mother-in-law visiting with a broom and scrub-bucket in hand.

A second daughter, Grace Harrington Eldredge, arrived in February of 1841, but Sara's happy, contented life would implode within a year. Although she should have read and questioned the papers Charley constantly asked her to sign, legally, her John Hancock was a formality. Refusing to sign them wouldn't have halted Charley's frenzied real estate speculating, or lessened Sara's liability, when a lawsuit was filed charging him with fraud.

Daughter Ellen Willis Eldredge was born in the midst of what would become a four-year legal ordeal. Seven-year-old Mary would die of brain fever (meningitis) before the judge ruled against Charley Eldredge.

Sara, already reeling from the death of her daughter, her mother, her sister Ellen, brother Nathaniel's wife, and two nephews, became a widow when Charley succumbed to typhoid four months after he'd lost his case in court.

Left with two young children and a mountain of debt, she moved to a tenement boardinghouse in Boston and took a seamstress job, earning at best, seventy-five cents a week.

Her in-laws refused to help financially—Charley's father was embroiled in his own speculative reversals, which his wife blamed on Sara. Deacon Willis grudgingly provided a small stipend and demanded she find a new husband to support her. Sara's brothers and sisters shunned her, as well, as Calvinism viewed bankruptcy as shameful, if not an outright sin.

The new breadwinner Deacon Willis handpicked for her was Samuel P. Farrington, a widower with two daughters of his own. Sara refused for a time, then after telling Samuel she didn't love him and was consenting for financial reasons, married him on January 17, 1846.

Her new husband, a demeaning, verbally abusive mirror image of Sara's father, was insanely jealous of her first husband, her friends, and anyone with whom she had contact. Every evening when he arrived home from work, his daughters reported what Sara had done that day, with whom she'd spoken, where she'd gone.

Five years later (almost to the day), Sara packed up and left him. Desertion and divorce were far more shameful and sinful than destitute widowhood, but Sara forged an iron-willed determination never again to rely on a man—any man—for a roof over her head or food on the table. She would, she declared, support herself with the only skill she felt she possessed: writing.

Olin Miller said, "Writing is the hardest way of earning a living with the possible exception of wrestling alligators." Sportswriter Red Smith disagreed (sort of): "Writing is easy; all you do is sit staring at a blank sheet of paper until the drops of blood form on your forehead." Sara likely experienced the latter and certainly related to the former, when she had to pester the *Olive Branch*'s editor for the grandiose fifty cents she earned for an anonymously printed essay. ". . . much pride I put in my pocket," she said, of her nascent career, "and few pennies."

Sara hoped her brother, Nathaniel Willis, editor of *Home Journal* (now *Town & Country* magazine), who'd published other struggling female writers, would lend similar assistance to her. She submitted to him the *Olive Branch* article and other writing samples.

The passages contained in his response that hurt and then incensed his younger sister the most were ". . . Your writings show talent, but . . . You overstrain the pathetic, and your humor runs into dreadful vulgarity sometimes. I am sorry that any editor knows that a sister of mine wrote some of these which you sent me."

The "dreadful vulgarity" to which Willis referred was not his younger sister's penchant for gutter-language. She dared suggest that marriage and motherhood weren't synonymous with heaven on earth. But biographer Warren maintains, the reasons he rejected Sara professionally and personally were professional and personal: She was unquestionably the better writer. In fact, some who wondered if he'd penned the articles Sara wrote anonymously remarked that if so, they were better than those written by N. P. Willis.

Nathaniel also feared that by association, Sara's dire financial straits and scandalous abandonment of her second husband could damage his social standing. Ironic, in light of Willis's prior excommunication from the church for his drinking and sexual exploits.

Having published several essays without signature, on September 6, 1851, the *Olive Branch* debuted Sara's first as Fanny Fern. *Fanny* may have been in tribute to the late writer Fanny Osgood, whom Sara admired, and she said she'd never met anyone by that name who wasn't fun to be around. *Fern* was an homage to her beloved mother and her affection for the fronds' sweet aroma.

The purpose of the nom de plume was a shield from her enemies, most particularly her estranged second husband. Its unexpected benefit was increasing publishing industry buzz surrounding the new satirist's gender (many guessed male) and true identity.

Readers couldn't care less. They clamored for more of Fanny Fern's honest, wry, down-to-earth point of view, whether they agreed with it or not. "Domestic humor," as two current feminist scholars aver, "provided a way for both writer and audience to minimize through laughter and, therefore, better cope with the frustrations and demands of their lives."

In June 1853, Fanny Fern's sketch titled, "Apollo Hyacinth" in *New York Musical World and Times* disavowed all notion that Nathaniel Willis might be freelancing under that pseudonym. Said to be the "not too friendly portrait of her brother, the poet journalist," New York insiders "had no difficulty recognizing N. P. Willis in [Apollo] the self-centered social climber and dandy portrayed in her sketch."

Willis evidently set no store by hell having no fury like a woman scorned, much less when she has a pen in hand and rapier wit.

By fall, Fanny Fern reprints began appearing in the *Home Journal,* while assistant editor James Parton filled in for ailing editor, Willis (his illness unspecified, but evidently genuine). Parton didn't know Fanny Fern was the boss's *persona non grata* sibling. He simply liked her writing, as did the *Journal's* readership.

When Willis recovered his health and the helm, he commanded Parton to cease using Fern's material. Parton refused, was cursed in a most ear-blistering manner, and then resigned.

In 1853, publishers Derby and Miller contacted Sara in regard to a book-length collection of columns. They offered a flat fee of one thousand dollars, or a dime royalty on each copy sold. Disregarding the adage about a bird in hand as opposed to two in the bush, she gambled on herself and accepted the royalty arrangement.

Titled *Fern Leaves from Fanny's Portfolio* (the woman was inordinately fond of alliteration) within months, the book's U.S. sales hit seventy thousand copies, with another twenty-nine thousand sold in Great Britain.

The reviews weren't universal raves, but brooked comparisons to Dickens and analogies that her satire was "keen as a razor." James Parton eloquently stated that Fanny Fern was "a voice, not an echo."

Charles Caleb Colton's contention that "imitation is the sincerest form of flattery" didn't hold a drop of water with Sara. England's Harry Honeysuckle's attempts at imitating her style were as infuriating to her as numerous publications here and abroad that pirated her work.

A second publishing contract for a children's book (*Little Ferns for Fanny's Little Friends*) and another essay collection *(Fern Leaves from Fanny's Portfolio, Second Series)* contained a clause ensuring both would be copyrighted in the U.S. and Great Britain.

Samuel Farrington, who'd recently obtained a divorce on grounds of desertion, declared Sara's earnings prior to the decree were joint marital assets and demanded his share. Nearly two and a half years had passed since she walked out, except the divorce was granted *days* before she signed the contract with Derby and Miller. She didn't owe Farrington a dime, let alone half of every one received for the book.

The verities were finally smiling on Sara—financially, as well as romantically. James Parton wasn't admiring of merely her writing, but of the writer herself, as well. The affection was mutual, but Sara was in no rush to find out if a third trip to the altar was charm, especially as "Jemmy" was eleven years her junior.

If those novels long ago hidden in her apron pocket were

sinful, her odds of salvation surely took a sharp nosedive when she wrote one. *Ruth Hall,* a diaphanously veiled roman a clef, was Apollo Hyacinth's encore, albeit renamed Hyacinth Elle. Pseudonymous characters also represented her long-suffering mother and her father, along with her Eldredge in-laws and virtually everyone whose Christian charity hadn't extended to Sara, or her little girls.

The publisher, Mason Brothers, launched an unprecedented promotional campaign. Curious to see what all the hubbub was about, no less a literary personage as Nathaniel Hawthorne wrote his publisher to "qualify his earlier criticism of the 'damned mob of scribbling women.'"

His comments, also contained in Warren's biography, must have levitated Sara above terra firma for several days:

> In my last [letter], I recollect, I bestowed some vituperation on female authors. I have since been reading "Ruth Hall"; and I must say I enjoyed it a good deal. The woman writes as if the devil was in her; and that is the only condition under which a woman ever writes anything worth reading. Generally women write like emasculated men, and are only distinguished from male authors by greater feebleness and folly; but when they throw off the restraint of decency, and come before the public stark naked, as it were—then their books are sure to possess character and value. Can you tell me anything about this Fanny Fern? If you meet her, I wish you would let her know how much I admire her.

Again, lest Hawthorne's references to "the devil in her" and "stark naked" infer that Sara's novel was Victorian soft porn, it was her revolutionary portrayal of the eponymous Ruth Hall as a free-thinking, nonconventional independent woman that he admired.

Which meant countless readers had copies tucked in *their* aprons, for the novel's sales outpaced other titles published at the same time, including Harriet Beecher Stowe's *Uncle Tom's Cabin*. Editors and reviewers who loathed Ruth Hall waxed vehement, yet their commentary boiled down to calling Fanny Fern an uppity female who didn't know her place, or had the audacity to step out of it.

Surprisingly, female reviewers also attacked the author, more so than the book. One, who knew Fanny Fern's true identity, disparaged her in a suffragette publication as having been "a poor housekeeper."

Sara seemed to take the potshots on the chin, then admitted years later that the personal assaults brought her to tears. Horatio Alger's stories of boys pulling themselves up by the proverbial bootstraps were lauded. To substitute *Ruth Hall* for *Ragged Dick* was profane.

Mary Kelley's *Private Woman, Public Stage* stresses the difference between Fanny Fern the essayist and humorist and Fanny Fern the novelist, as a dual identity. The first, straightforward, satirical, yet commonsensical; the second was more conventional, florid, sentimental, closer to what Kelley called a "literary domestic" and Hawthorne dubbed "the mob of scribbling women."

It was Sara's lived-in-parlor voice, where thumbprints smudged the doorjamb and gingersnap crumbs speckled the floor, that editor Robert Bonner of the *New York Ledger* paid an unprecedented hundred dollars per column to print. As of

January 12, 1856, she was the highest-paid newspaper columnist in America, author of four best-selling books and the newly-wedded bride of James Parton.

Her second novel, *Rose Clark*, was another roman à clef centering on the humiliation and escape from her marriage to Samuel Farrington.

In some respects, *Rose Clark* wasn't as well written as its predecessor. The prose was choppier, the transitions abrupt, or nonexistent, yet early reviews were less caustic. Both novels were social commentaries woven into fictional form; but perhaps it was more palatable to condemn a cruel, abusive spouse than one's father and brother.

The *New York Times*, however, damned the book with no praise whatsoever. The review's most revealing aspect, Joyce W. Warren states, is its "denunciation of a woman for mentioning—even to a female friend—the horror of being used sexually by a husband who degraded and mistreated her and for whom she felt neither love nor respect."

Fanny Fern's column continued to appear weekly in the *Ledger*, but she produced no more novels. Maybe she realized the personal essay was the bullier pulpit. Maybe she'd run out of autobiographical axes to grind. Whatever the reason, it wasn't because a weekly column was an easier, faster format.

Contrary to assumption, a short article takes considerably longer to write than the finished product does to read. As any contemporary essayist would attest, for every somewhat mythical column that "writes itself" are dozens that make coal mining seem a less laborious vocation. And Fanny Fern composed hers by hand and met deadlines via courier even before express mail was of the pony variety.

In sixteen years, she never missed a deadline. Not when her daughter Grace died of scarlet fever, three weeks after giving Sara her first grandchild. Not when she and James took responsibility for parenting Grace's baby, Grace Ethel Thompson. Not when her own "contest with death" began, as James described Sara's refusal to let on to anyone, other than her immediate family, that she was dying of cancer.

A year before her death, surgery to halt the spread of the disease paralyzed her right arm. Sara gripped the pen in her left hand and composed the week's column. When it fell useless, she dictated them to James or to her daughter Ellen.

The pain was unrelenting, but she refused to give in, even after she became too weak to walk. The tone and content of her work was as consistent as it had been for sixteen years.

Fanny Fern's October 12, 1872, column outlived its creator by two days. Due to the *Ledger's* publishing schedule, newspapers nationwide printed eulogies and tributes three weeks before Robert Bonner's black-boxed editorial of November 2, 1872.

"The Child Whom Nobody Can Do Anything With" grew up to become in many ways, the nation's diarist, its conscience, and its sense of humor, when laughter was most needed.

Additional column collections were titled: *Fresh Leaves* (1857), *Folly as it Flies* (1868), *Ginger Snaps* (1870), and *Caper-Sauce,* (1872).

(Author's collection)

15

LYDIA PINKHAM

*In certain diseases, the scientific physician, with the aid of the
microscope, &c., may be enabled to give an accurate diagnosis,
but with the patient, the* remedy *is the thing.*

Much fun was poked at Lydia E. Pinkham's Vegetable
Compound in her day. The gibes might have continued
until the present, had the housewife-chemist and her product
remained as famous as in their heyday. But it's doubtful that
many, if any, elixirs first marketed in 1875 are still in production
and available on Internet drugstore sites.

Lydia was William and Rebecca Estes's tenth child, born on
February 2, 1819, near Lynn, Massachusetts. The farthest Lydia
would travel from that small community, about twenty miles
from Boston, would be the few years she'd live in Bedford, approximately thirty miles from her hometown.

Lydia's ancestors included one Mary Tyler, who in 1692 was
condemned to death as a witch for the writhing, torturous af-

flictions she allegedly twitched up on Timothy Swan, a rejected suitor. Happily, witch-burning was falling out of vogue, and Mary was later acquitted and received monetary damages from the court for her false imprisonment.

Lydia's parents and forebears had been members of the Society of Friends, but William and Rebecca soon left the Quaker fold. The church's division over abolition and the Estes's friendship with neighbor Frederick Douglass contributed to the decision.

Lydia attended grammar school and later, the Lynn Academy, having decided to become a schoolteacher. She'd already taught Frederick Douglass's wife to read—which he may later have regretted, as after the Civil War, he was an outspoken opponent to the women's voting rights movement.

In September 1843, the tall (at feet seven inches), red-haired Lydia married Isaac Pinkham, a real estate speculator convinced that railroad service would trigger a boom in land values.

The newlyweds settled in Wynoma Village on the outskirts of Lynn in a house nicknamed Old Lightning-Splitter, for its steep-pitched roof. In time, Isaac's property acquisitions made him the richest man in the area, albeit on paper, not in cash. Lydia gave birth to four sons, with three surviving: Charles, Daniel, and William Henry. Their fourth child and only daughter, Aroline, was born in Bedford, where the Pinkhams moved after Isaac suffered "financial reversals."

Her motto was, "A sure six-pence is better than a doubtful shilling,"—a shade of the more commonly and less numismatically oriented "A bird in hand is worth two in the bush." However said, it's evident Isaac didn't share the same credo.

Wherever they lived and whatever the state of their finances, Lydia became a neighborhood visiting volunteer nurse. Many of the nostrums (the original Latin means "our own") she dispensed had been passed down through the family. Others, she developed from an interest in and constant reading about pharmacology, medicinal theories, general practices, and advancements. Throughout her life, she clipped or copied items of interest and collected them in a scrapbook.

She also dismissed any number of noted practitioners' views as pure balderdash, if not outright homicide. One important exception was Dr. Oliver Wendell Holmes's revolutionary and much-ridiculed ideas on the existence of contagions and that doctors should wash their hands frequently with calcium chloride—at the very least, a vigorous scrub with soap.

Some years would pass before a correlation between the higher survival rate of infants (and postpartum mothers) delivered by prescrubbed midwives (Lydia included) and those left in the dirty-nailed, grubby hands of unwashed "doctors."

Lydia was significantly unimpressed by all areas of medical treatment afforded her gender. "It is a very sad fact that the more a woman trusts to the skill of her physician in treating her female complaints, the longer she is apt to suffer."

Neither sex was immune from mid-nineteenth-century contradictions to Hippocrates' "First do no harm." Standard treatments included bleeding (draining blood from incision to the wrist), blistering (cauterizing), and leeching (applying maggots to devour inflamed/infected tissue).

Medicinal treatments favored nux-vomica (strychnine), opium, quinine, antimony, and the all-purpose calomel, a blend of two toxins: metallic mercury and corrosive sublimate.

Lydia favored the so-called eclectic practice of medicine

which relied on botanical remedies. Simples, as they were called, were topical salves, creams, and balms of various persuasions. Medicinals were ingestibles made from roots, leaves, herbs, and were often brewed into teas.

To help her nonpaying but never-ending clientele requesting her nursing services, Lydia mixed up a batch of vegetable compound developed by eclectic practitioner Dr. John King, which was contained in his book titled, *The American Dispensary*.

The women who tried it reported a marked improvement in health. Soon word of mouth had others knocking at Lydia's door asking for a bottle—for which she refused to charge a penny.

To her mind, taking money for the compound was akin to guests paying for the tea and cookies she served.

In 1872, Isaac's fortunes had rerisen to the point he moved the family to the biggest, nicest house in Wyoma. A fountain was installed on the front lawn, and daughter Aroline practiced scales on a spanking-new grand piano.

Alas, his net worth remained in the form of property titles and cosigning friends' promissory notes on their speculative parcels. His house of real estate cards, which could have netted a fortune, toppled asunder during the panic of '73. One week before he and Lydia celebrated their thirtieth wedding anniversary, they were stone-broke.

After a move to a smaller house in the oldest part of town, a family meeting was held around the dining room table, as was the Pinkhams' custom. Rather than dinnertime philosophical and political discussions, they brainstormed a solution to their dire financial straits. Based on the stranger in a carriage who'd recently stopped at the house for six bottles of the compound (which Lydia reluctantly accepted five dollars for), they determined the formula was their only asset.

In all-for-one, one-for-all fashion, they voted to share the work and the profits, assuming there ever were any. Every possible penny would be pinched from household expenses to offset start-up costs.

In addition to production, Lydia took charge of advertising. Handbills were composed, and labels were created. A multipage brochure was written titled "Guide for Women" and was chock-full of her common-sense advice. Every piece of advertisement invited customers to "write to Mrs. Lydia E. Pinkham, Lynn, Massachusetts."

Although not given to bragging, judging by the testimonials of those who'd used the compound, Lydia headlined the literature: *The Greatest Medical Discovery Since the Dawn of History*.

It was also, by subsequent handbills, a liquid self-defense against spousal homicide. "A FEARFUL TRAGEDY," began one tract. "A Clergyman of Stratford, Connecticut, KILLED BY HIS OWN WIFE, Insanity Brought on by 16 Years of Suffering with FEMALE COMPLAINTS THE CAUSE." Now that a reader's attention was likely riveted, the text went on, "Lydia E. Pinkham's Vegetable Compound, The Sure Cure for These Complaints, Would Have Prevented the Direful Deed."

Long a devotee of cleanliness and hygiene, Lydia scrubbed and sanitized the kitchen-cum-laboratory in the cellar to within an inch of its life. Soon, the upper rooms filled with fumes from pots of her miraculous compound.

The ingredients were measured on a kitchen scale: 8 ounces, true unicorn root (alestris); 8 ounces, false unicorn root (chamaelirium luteum); 6 ounces life root (golden ragwort); 6

ounces black cohosh; 6 ounces pleurisy root (asclepias); 12 ounces fenugreek seed (Trigonella foenum graecum L.).

Some were steeped in water or diluted alcohol; some soaked in cold water. All were combined and strained through cloth, similar to the process for homemade fruit jelly.

Except Grandma's wild plum jelly didn't pack an 18 percent alcohol-punch, as the vegetable compound did after being cut with a generous dollop as a dilutant and preservative. Not enough, however, to prevent the Women's Christian Temperance Union from wholeheartedly endorsing the elixir.

Aside from Isaac, who read aloud to the crew, everyone pitched in after supper to fill and cork the bottles of finished product and pack them in used grocery boxes for shipping.

Products were sold to druggists on a consignment basis. The nationwide financial panic had not abated, and merchants couldn't afford to invest in inventory that might gather dust on the shelves.

Lydia's sons had shingled the surrounding countryside with handbills promoting the elixir, but Daniel knew a far wider customer base was needed to turn a profit. The fledgling company's singular sales force struck out for New York, distributing literature as fast as it was printed.

Some biographical references interpret the record Daniel kept of out-of-pocket expenses to be moneys Lydia charged her adult live-at-home son for meals and rent. Rather, his ledgers were almost certainly a means of tracking the company's out-go versus income, just as wise business owners do today. He also dickered on printing expenses, pitting one printer's cost-per-thousand (then upwards of ten thousand) against another, which he'd have had difficulty doing without written records.

One of Daniel's letters home expresses his frustration and answers complaints about a perceived lack of communication: "I think I write pretty confounded often. I know it costs a pile for stamps, postal cards and paper. I guess I'll go to bed now, I'm pretty tired tonight. I'm at work early and late . . . What do you think, will the business pay or not? I sometimes feel as if I didn't know."

Druggists in that city were as tight-fisted as in Massachusetts. He divined the idea to leave free samples that, when sold, would motivate shopkeepers to become sales agents and stock the compound in quantity.

While Dan Pinkham's shoeleather sales campaign wasn't exactly taking New York by storm, Lydia was using testimonials from letters she received to lengthen the list of ailments treated, relieved and cured by her elixir: kidney complaints, uterine complaints, back trouble, spinal weakness, faintness, flatulency, bloating, headaches, nervous prostration, general debility, sleeplessness, depression, and indigestion.

Now fifty-seven years old, Lydia also cared for Isaac, a semi-invalid, managed the household, the laboratory, and shipping operation—all with calm, capable efficiency. References to regularly dosing herself with the compound weren't found, but with or without the elixir, she obviously had more stamina than women half her age.

It was Dan, a natural-born publicist, whose stroke of genius put his mother's photograph on all Pinkham literature. From bottle labels to brochures it was the first use of a photograph in advertising.

Lydia dressed for the occasion in a black silk dress, white, lace-trimmed triangular scarf pinned with a cameo brooch.

Her white hair, parted at center and caught up above her nape by tortoiseshell combs portrayed the epitome of a "dream grandmother."

Photos of the well-scrubbed cellar laboratory were also incorporated as illustrations. The allusion to homemade products underscored a feeling of intimacy with her customers, and her spotless lab-keeping was the antithesis of many apothecary shops of the day:

Laggards slouched about, eyeballing female customers, making frequent but wildly off-target use of the spittoons, or less troublesome, the floor. Doors open as weather permitted welcomed insects, dust, and gusts of eau de manure. Measuring utensils, mortars, and pestles might be rinsed at day's end. Thumbs were employed to wipe spills from bottles, and pharmacists were about as scrupulous about handwashing as doctors were.

In 1876, Lydia registered her labels with the U.S. Patent Office, but intentionally did not patent the formula. By law, the labels' brand name, slogan, and so forth, was renewable every twenty years, whereas a patent on the compound would expire in seventeen years and become public domain.

Her formula or a facsimile thereof, could be duplicated, but no one could produce Lydia E. Pinkham's Vegetable Compound other than Mrs. Pinkham, her heirs, and assigns.

Not patenting the formula also allowed for changes, in the event Lydia ever chose to, or was forced to, by an inability to procure the ingredients. As it was, true unicorn and pleurisy root hadn't been listed in the United States Pharmacopoeia since 1835.

Second thoughts about the alcohol content—or customer complaints—might have induced an alteration. According to an article by Gerald Carson, Dr. Samuel B. Hartman was notified by the United States Treasury department that unless he could prove his nostrum "Peruna" had a medicinal effect, he'd be taxed as an alcoholic beverage purveyor.

The good doctor and former Bible salesman added a heaping helping of blackthorn bark (a powerful, effective laxative) to his original recipe. "There followed a national rumbling of bowels that was heard from Maine to California."

The Pinkhams were still plowing most of the profits back into the business, but orders had picked up dramatically. Deciding it time to come out of the cellar, Lydia leased the house next door. After the owner finished the necessary remodeling, she opened the facility to public tours on weekdays, from 8 A.M. to 4 P.M. (another probable first).

Thus far, the company's advertising had relied on handbills, brochures, and word of mouth. Dan believed the time had come for newspaper advertising. A front-page box in the Boston *Herald* cost sixty dollars (a typical postman's monthly salary), but in a fell swoop, it introduced thousands of people to The Greatest Medical Discovery Since the Dawn of History.

Another family meeting approved mortgaging the house as collateral for one thousand dollars' worth of *Herald* advertising. That gamble seemed completely out of character for Lydia, particularly in light of Isaac's speculative disasters and the panic's enduring economic recession, but it paid for itself in increased orders.

Unfortunately, the tireless salesman and brilliant promoter fell ill in 1879. Lydia tried every treatment in her arsenal, but Dan's nagging cough developed into tuberculosis. Massachusetts winters being brutal on healthy lungs, he repaired to Georgia and later, west to Texas.

The notes Lydia enclosed with each shipment, all beginning "Dear Friend" and ending, "Yours for Health," became more than she could handle, along with bagfuls of correspondence. A team of female secretarial assistants was employed to hand-copy Lydia's prewritten responses to virtually any type of inquiry.

Dan Pinkham returned to Lynn in 1881, looking by no means as though he'd "bankrupted a rainbow," as his family had hoped. He died that October at the age of thirty-two. Lydia and Isaac were heartbroken, yet, she realized, his death emphasized an oversight that must be amended.

Dan's share of the profits were divided equally among his brothers and sister. Aroline's fiancé, attorney William Gove, then drew up the paperwork for Lydia E. Pinkham and Company. All profits of the company would be divided between Isaac, Lydia, and their children, a formal record of their original agreement.

Tragically, their twenty-eight-year-old son, Will, contracted tuberculosis, as well. He and his wife, Emma, left immediately for California, but it was too late. Unlike his brother, Will was what was termed "a quick consumptive." He died in Los Angeles less than two months after Dan.

The company underwent another reorganization as Lydia E. Pinkham Medicine Company. Its 112 shares were divided: 49 each for surviving son, Charles, and daughter, Aroline, who gave one share to husband William Gove, allowing him a seat on the board of directors, and 14 shares for Emma Pinkham, Will's widow.

In the manner of tragedies occurring in threes, Emma Pinkham succumbed to tuberculosis in 1882. As she and Will had no children, there was some anxiety about her parents inheriting her fourteen company shares. Well-founded anxiety, as the directors would soon discover.

Apparently the public saw more than a vegetable compound's namesake in that "dream grandmother's" visage. As a dispenser of health advice, Lydia excelled, but an increasing number of correspondents were girls and young women seeking answers to questions they'd never dare ask their own mothers or grandmothers.

The volume of mail inspired Lydia to write a book titled "Yours for Health" and "Married Women and Those About to Be." She charged not a penny, averring, "The women of this country must have physical education, if we are to have a people strong and hearty."

The books not only provided answers to delicate questions, but also contained illustrations of "The Female Pelvis" and the precise nature of puberty, ovulation, conception, birth, and menopause, of which (unbelievably or not) a majority of both sexes were entirely ignorant. Lydia even stated categorically that sterility was by no means entirely the fault of the woman, that many men were sterile, but blamed perpetually empty cradles on their wives.

According to biographer Jean Burton, Lydia's books "remained the only work of its kind available for free distribution, until the government began issuing its bulletins on prenatal and post-partum care, child-training, and so on . . ."

Of course, some of the letters Lydia received were pranks. Fraternity boys were known to write under a female nom de-plume asking for advice on curing frigidity and similar sex-oriented topics.

Charles Pinkham, now in charge of promotions by default, if not design, hired a professional agent named (by one account) Elbert Hubbard, to expand and monitor a national newspaper advertising campaign. Later, and by pure chance, Charles found what he believed was a double-billing error on the part of the Boston *Globe*.

Inspecting the newspaper records probably triggered a queasiness his mother's nostrum wouldn't assuage. The records were correct. Elbert Hubbard was buying advertising space in big blocks, presumably charged to the Pinkham account, then at an inflated price, sold them back to create a running line of credit.

By so doing and in multiple, Hubbard effectively became the company's largest creditor. At any moment, he could call in those markers and take over the company.

Following the agent's footsteps from Maine to California and points south and southwest, Charles cancelled ads at every stop and issued promissory notes for the unpaid balances. It's said that in one afternoon, he signed forty-three notes at one thousand dollars each. When finished, the company was $125,000 in the red.

The ad cancellations caused a precipitous slump in orders, but Charles vowed to repay every dollar he'd promised. As for Hubbard's malfeasance, Charles impulsively settled for ten thousand dollars in damages, reportedly the first number that popped into his head.

Not long after, Hubbard informed the company's directors that he also owned the fourteen shares passed to Emma Pinkham's parents after her death.

Two days before Christmas in 1882, Lydia was felled by a stroke and left partially paralyzed. Ofttimes her slurred speech was nonsensical—torture for an intelligent, articulate woman. Over the next five months, she'd rally a bit, raising her and her family's hopes for a recovery, then weaken.

The company she'd started in the cellar of her home and worked tirelessly to build was grossing three hundred thousand dollars the year Lydia died, 1883. In a not particularly surprising show of poor taste, Hubbard, the scurrilous publicity agent, came to the funeral bearing an enormous floral arrangement. It's a wonder one of the Pinkhams didn't put it, as they say, where the sun don't shine.

Four years later, Charles bought back Hubbard's shares and the company soldiered on without its founder and namesake. Squabbles among extended family members erupted, as is often the case. One of Lydia's grandsons, a medical student and amateur chemist, reproduced and repackaged the formula as Delmac Vegetable Compound, spurring yet another reorganization.

In 1902, *Ladies' Home Journal*, which had prohibited patent medicine advertisements for decades, published an exposé of the nostrums in general and various brands in particular, including Lydia E. Pinkham's Vegetable Compound.

In few uncertain terms, the article keyed on current company advertising that implied Mrs. Pinkham was still personally answering correspondence addressed to her in Lynn, Massachusetts. An adjacent photograph of her headstone at Pine Grove Cemetery, graven with her name and date of death, needed no caption to clarify the point.

Ten years earlier, the *Journal*'s editor, Edward Bok, was the target of a practical joke played by friend and *Chicago Daily News* columnist, Eugene Field. Aware that Bok detested the very idea of patent medicines and, perhaps, it being a slow news day in the Windy City, Field composed a story announcing the engagement of Edward Bok to the fetching and wealthy Miss Lavinia Pinkham, the nonexistent granddaughter of the queen of alcoholic vegetable compounds. When the piece evidently escaped Bok's notice, Field tapped out a sequel regarding the starry-eyed couple's clandestine voyage to Paris to shop for Miss Pinkham's trousseau.

An avalanche of letters and telegrams from patent medicine companies piled Bok's desk, on the assumption the *Journal's* editor had undergone a literal change of heart. If or how the besieged Edward Bok retaliated against his waggish friend isn't known, but the Pinkham heirs and assigns undoubtedly got a good laugh out of the hoax.

Before World War I, the company expanded internationally, grossing a reported four million dollars in 1925. Toward the end of World War II, an Army chaplain was astonished to discover in one snapshot he'd taken of a recently liberated South Sea island, a native woman, standing in front of her thatched hut, had a clearly visible bottle of Lydia E. Pinkham's Vegetable Compound.

In the March 15, 2001, issue of *Family Practice News*, the opening line reads: *Lydia Pinkham had the right idea.* While her nostrum wasn't a cure-all for the myriad diseases and conditions her early customers avowed, its infusion of black cohosh has been determined an effective treatment for menstrual and menopausal symptoms.

The article, written by Nancy Walsh, states that German clinical trials found "... black cohosh to be superior to placebo;" a conclusion seconded by Dr. Victoria E. Rand at a "conference on alternative and complementary medicine sponsored by the University of Chicago."

As for Lydia Pinkham's Vegetable Compound, Dr. Rand

said, "Women really raved about this stuff," adding, in regard to its 18 percent alcohol content, "There was more to it than just the black cohosh."

Numark Laboratories, manufacturers of products ranging from Bromo-seltzer to Aquacare Lotion for Dry Skin, acquired the rights to the Lydia Pinkham brand in the 1960s. The "dream grandmother's" photograph still adorns the packaging, though it's been reformulated as an herbal liquid supplement, rather than a vegetable compound with a high-octane alcohol kick.

While not so commonly found on drugstore and supermarket shelves as other Numark products, a bottle can easily be purchased from a variety of Internet vendors.

"Day in and day out, she toils," said Lydia Pinkham, 135 years ago, continuing:

> She is the bread-winner of the family, and must work that others may live . . . Six o'clock—weary women watch for that blessed hour. On the stroke of six ends the day's work at stores, offices, factories, mills where women are employed. But their necessary work at home—sewing, mending, etc.,—must be done *after* that time, for "woman's work is never done."

From a nineteenth-century home-cellar-based business to e-commerce, the more some things change, it seems, the more others remain the same.

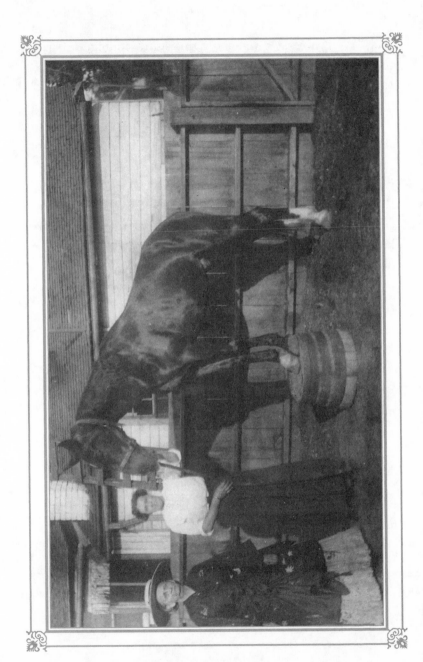

Mattie Silks and her own horse

16

MATTIE SILKS

A most disgraceful row occurred late on Friday night.
Two notorious women of the town, Mattie Silks
and Katie Fulton, were principals . . .

—*Denver News*, 1877

The answer to the perpetual "What do you want to be when you grow up?" is dependent upon the age of the respondent. As often as not, little kids' sights set on police officer, mermaid, ballerina, or rock star. By late adolescence, a career choice is likely tailored to sound dandy to adult ears—such as doctor, lawyer, architect, business administrator, who'd be less than impressed by a truthful, "Jeez, I don't have a clue."

It's presumed that Martha (Mattie) Silks was neither asked nor volunteered her ambition to become a parlor house madam, but by various accounts, her mind was made up by the time she was fourteen or so.

The type of establishment she intended to own represented

the top rung of the prostitution ladder. A parlor house served a higher and wealthier class of customers, thus the decor was tastefully opulent, the piano player ("the professor") was musically inclined, the liquor and cigars were the finest money could buy, and the demimondaines exceptionally lovely to look at, well-spoken, and cultured—perfect ladies, as it were, aside from being practitioners of the world's oldest profession.

Bordellos ranked a few notches below a parlor house. A middle-manager level, as it were, as opposed to a CEO's. Some of them slid further down the socioeconomic scale, but were still ranked above a brothel. Brothels were often located above a saloon or dance hall and catered to working men, drifters—generally anyone with ten bucks in his pocket and a yen for temporary female companionship.

The term *hog-ranch* is pretty self-explanatory. Many were mobile, in that they followed military units from camp to camp and plied their trade in tents. These "brides of the multitudes" had either de-escalated in looks and earning power (if they'd ever enjoyed either) from bordello to brothel to camp-follower, or had simply started at the bottom and stayed there.

Noms de plume also distinguished the parlor house girls from their sisters in bordellos and even poorer establishments. Tit Bit, Peg-Leg, Galloping Cow, and Hambone Jane, for example, were doves considerably more soiled than a Jenny or a Cassie—let alone a Veronique or a Katherine.

Where or how Mattie Silks was inspired to curry to the carriage trade isn't known, though at that time other than marrying money, owning a parlor house was a woman's best and fastest route to Easy Street.

She was born in about 1846 on a Kansas farm, or in the

vicinity of Terra Haute, Indiana, or Buffalo, New York. None were a hop, skip, and a jump from Springfield, Illinois, where Mattie was running a "female boarding house" by the age of nineteen.

Springfield might seem like an odd place to start, but like the 1961 spring-break/beach movie, Mattie set up shop "Where The Boys Are." The town was almost smack in the middle of Illinois, hence a crossroads leading to or from Indianapolis, Chicago, St. Louis, and Kansas City. With the Civil War in its last throes, if not over, Mattie's palace of consolation and pleasure was undoubtedly a popular way-stop for soldiers passing through town.

Throughout her life she boasted (perhaps a few times too many) that she never personally purveyed her charms to her clientele. True or not, with curly blond hair and cornflower blue eyes, she was said to be a somewhat shorter spittin' image of actress Lily Langtry—the Victorian Angelina Jolie. Always attired in the latest fashions, Mattie did the designers one better by having two hidden pockets sewn in her gowns. One held gold coins. The other, according to one source, was where she stashed an "ivory-handled pistol." That last is probably an exaggeration.

A standard revolver would be akin to carrying a long-barreled brick in her pocket, and the lighter, so-called Suicide Specials weren't manufactured until close to 1900.

An ivory grip harks a dueling pistol; a single-shot, more cumbersome weapon and probably a hindsighted derivative of her legendary stand-up shootout with Katie Fulton. Being "heeled" as a woman in her business surely was, Mattie was more likely armed with a fancy derringer (pepperbox), as whomever she might intend to ventilate would be in close and deadly proximity.

Paraphrasing Horace Greeley's famed manifest destination, "Go west, young madam" was precisely what Mattie did, arriving in Denver City in 1876. Several parlor houses were established along Holladay (Market) Street from the 1900 block to 2000. She also reportedly franchised her houses in Georgetown and Leadville, Colorado, and as far away as Dawson, Canada, but would have had her hands quite full managing her pleasure palaces in Denver City.

As a madam, Mattie essentially strawbossed a chain of upscale hotels with somewhat limited hours of operation. Maids in her employ changed bed linens after each use, kept the parlors and rooms tidy at all times, as well as handled the daily dusting, polishing, and carpet-sweeping.

Crystal barware must be spotlessly kempt. Liquor and cigars ordered and stocked, as well as the pantry, where the kitchen help prepared and served the girls two excellent daily meals.

There were bribes and license fees to pay, along with the house bouncer and the professor—positions subject to a fairly high turnover rate. Mattie was also the girls' mother-confessor and kept a sharp eye peeled for signs of depression, alcoholism, drug use, and disease.

Rotating her stable's available inventory and adding new faces was an ongoing process. Mattie didn't recruit off the street and certainly didn't engage in white slavery (kidnapping young girls and forcing them into the trade), but traveled East every year in search of new girls.

The cheapest and most effective method of advertising was the girls' (new and established) taking an afternoon stroll, dressed in their finest and, typically, with a poodle tucked in their arms. The breed became so associated with Cyprians that no decent lady dared own one.

Considering Mattie's knowledge of the masculine psyche and propensities, one would think she'd have pegged Cortez "Cort" Thomson as a bounder from the get-go. Instead, she fell head over heels in love with the fleet foot-racer, who sprinted from here to yonder in a pair of pink tights and star-spangled blue trunks.

Cort supposedly rode with Quantrill's raiders during the Civil War, his athletic ability an adjunct to being shot, stabbed, or captured in the process of committing multiple felonies.

Phyllis Flanders Dorset's, *The New Eldorado*, describes the love of Mattie Silks's life as "a Texan of medium height, blue of eye, virile, handsome, with sandy hair and a copper-tinctured mustache." What money Cort earned gambling on himself in foot-races didn't finance his love of the finer things in life. Mattie, however, was willing, able, and happy to provide.

Cort was married and had a daughter, as well as a mistress with an apparent deep coin-pocket in her dress, but it didn't put blinders on his roving eye. While Mattie may have been aware of Cort's casual indiscretions, he became a mite too interested in another madam named Katie Fulton.

A business rival combined with a romantic rival was more than Mattie could take. Logic dictates that Cort Thomson would be kicked to the boardwalk, *tont de suite*. Mattie, infatuated beyond reason, instead challenged Katie to a duel.

Or so maintains approximately half the available accounts on the subject. The balance swears the shoot-out was a figment of writer Forbes Parkhill's vivid imagination. Not that one should take as gospel everything one reads in a newspaper, but both the *Denver Post* and *Rocky Mountain News* reported on the .38-caliber catfight.

The site of the alleged duel, Olympic Gardens, was a public park and botanical garden just outside Denver City proper, thus beyond its police force's jurisdiction. Stretching out from the Platte's shady west bank, the amusements included a picnic pavilion, a freak museum, a mineral exhibit, and a zoo featuring indigenous Colorado wildlife.

Although signs proclaimed somewhat vaguely, NO IMPROPER CHARACTERS PERMITTED!, there was no express prohibition against two well-dressed parlor house madams squaring off in an open, grassy area for the purpose of winning Cort Thomson's obviously fickle affections.

Mattie and Katie adhered more-or-less to the Code Duello, with Cort acting as Mattie's second and Sam Thatcher as Katie's. It isn't clear how many yards the women put between them, or which (if either) second signaled "Fire!" but their respective pistols definitely blazed.

There's a rather marvelous poetic justice in the pro-duel accounts that the clearing powder-smoke found Katie and Mattie still standing and unhurt, and Cort Thomson writhing in the grass from a gunshot wound to the neck.

Since the duelers' prowess with firearms was equally poor, it couldn't be determined which one nicked Cort instead of her presumed intended target. To Mattie went the spoils, as Katie Fulton fled Denver City, in case Cort's wound turned mortal and Mattie's marksmanship improved.

Cort survived and was cockier than ever. He'd gallop his horse up Mattie's front steps and through the door to demand money, yet, Lord love him, bought her a diamond-studded cross with some of it.

When his wife died, he even did the gentlemanly thing and proposed to Mattie. Following an engagement party at (where else?) the Olympic Gardens, the pink-tighted, star-spangled sprinter married the madam with a penchant for silk and lace gowns reminiscent of Catherine de' Medici.

Two years later, Cort received word that his daughter had died, leaving a child. When he refused to take responsibility for his granddaughter, Mattie adopted the girl. A parlor house not being a particularly good environment for a growing girl, Mattie paid a respectable couple to board and care for the child; the customary arrangement for prostitutes with children.

Contrary to then-conventional wisdom, professional courtesans possessed no secret birth-control devices, or measures that held Mother Nature at bay. Pregnancy and venereal disease were their greatest fears. Douching with a diluted carbolic acid, mercuric chloride, or alum had a degree of effectiveness. Some discovered regularly using opiates disrupted or stopped the menstrual cycle.

Strangely, many of their johns' wives weren't ignorant of their husbands patronizing houses of ill repute. Not that they approved, but prostitutes were a defacto birth control device for women who loved their spouses dearly, but perished the thought of bearing a child every year or so.

By 1890, newcomers to town and passers-through could contact Mattie Silks by phone at 6255, which was on the city's main exchange. Two years later, the *Denver Red Book: A Reliable Directory of the Pleasure Resorts of Denver* was published and available citywide. In 1900, the census listed Mattie as a landlady renting to female boarders aged nineteen to twenty-five, which got the message across with utmost discretion.

Sadly, that same year, Cort Thomson lost his race with the Grim Reaper. Mattie threw one of the most lavish funerals the city had ever seen, but was nearly prostrate with grief. The rake hadn't worked a day since they met. He'd reportedly gambled or otherwise frittered away fifty thousand dollars of her money. But she loved him with all her heart.

Described as "well-upholstered," when she'd arrived in Denver City, as her girth expanded, her beauty diminished. Still, she caught the eye of "Handsome" Jack Ready, a strapping bouncer several years her junior. Jack eventually became her financial manager, except before long, Mattie and the rest of the denizens of the tenderloin district wouldn't have businesses to manage.

A crusader named George Creel was appointed police commissioner in 1913 and vowed to clean up the city, with an assist from Sheriff Glen Duffield. Prostitution was outlawed in 1913. The following year, voters approved an amendment prohibiting liquor—the measure garnering statewide approval in 1916. The area once euphemized as Paradise Alley was redubbed Padlock Alley.

Jack Ready and Mattie married in 1923, but her sunset years were brief. As opposed to the send-off given her first husband, the eighty-three-year-old former madam's funeral in 1929 was quiet, with no flowers and no choir singing.

She was buried in Fairmount Cemetery beside her beloved Cort Thomson, though her headstone reads MATTIE READY. It was estimated she'd reaped two million dollars or more from the profession she chose as a teenager. The four thousand dollars, jewelry, and few parcels of property that comprised her estate were divided between Jack Ready and her adopted granddaughter.

When Jack died two years later, his friends passed a hat to pay for his burial.

Mattie Silks's business wasn't respectable. She didn't fit the image of the stereotypical whore with the heart of gold, either, but perhaps a bit of slack is warranted. The era in which she lived was considerably less than kind to the purported weaker sex, and the opposite gender has never been judged as harshly for frequenting a pleasure palace as have the women paid to provide it.

Silver Heels (Illustration by Zachary Ledbetter)

17

SILVER HEELS

When the facts fit the legend, print the legend.

—*THE MAN WHO SHOT LIBERTY VALANCE*
(BASED ON A SHORT STORY BY
DOROTHY M. JOHNSON)

On several levels, the word *shady* fits the Colorado dance hall denizen called Silver Heels. Her Christian name is lost to time, other than allusions that it may have been Bechtel, or perhaps Silber.

Her vocation was on the shady side as well, since dance hall girls tended to be round-heeled, whether they wore fancy dancing shoes or not.

Lastly, the terms fits the legend she left in her wake and its various endings; among them, frequent sightings of her in the mining camp's cemetery, both in corporeal and apparition form.

The emergence of the facts, as too many have attested for the entire story to be bushwah, begins circa 1859 and features a

prospector named "Buckskin Joe" Higgenbottom (or Higgan-
bottom, or Higgenbotham).

"Buckskin Joe" was one of the thousands of '59ers drawn to
Colorado Territory by news of gold strikes richer than those
ten years earlier in California.

Darned if Higgenbottom didn't find a pocket of placer gold
in Park County, seventy miles west of Denver and near the
mining camps of Fairplay and Alma.

Strikes being impossible to keep secret—if for no other reason, because of the necessity of assaying the gold and staking
claims—the word of Buckskin Joe's discovery whispered
through the aspen leaves.

A second alleged lode was stumbled upon by a poor
prospector but excellent hunter named Harrison, who'd winged
a deer in the same general vicinity. Out of sympathy for the
wounded animal, or visions of his larrupin' fresh venison supper skedaddling into the brush, Harrison tracked the buck by
its blood trail. Lo and behold, what he found was a rock
gouged by his stray bullet and an exposed vein of gold.

Harrison worked his mine in secret, lugging the spoils away
from the site and caching them for posterity. Eventually, his
buddies back in camp got curious about Harrison's daily dawn-
to-dusk hunting trips that suddenly weren't bagging a bite of
meat. The next morning, they allowed him a head start and
then tracked him to his clandestine mine.

This version of the jackpot is also attributed to Buckskin Joe
Higgenbottom, though sources say Harrison must truly have
been a sharper hunter than an argonaut, for he figured his
strike was on the surface and sold his claim to a Mr. Phillips.

Phillips subsequently reaped a cool, subterranean couple of million in gold from Dead-Eye Harrison's error in judgment.

An excerpt from a later issue of the *Denver Daily Tribune* said

> ... the remarkable mineral discoveries in Buckskin gulch drew an immense number of miners to that locality, and a busy bustling mining town of two thousand soon spring up. . . . miners and prospectors kept coming in from there [California gulch] at the rate of seventy-five to a hundred and twenty-five a day.

Under the new district's mining laws, "which were as faithfully observed as if they had been lawfully inscribed in the [Colorado Territory's] statute books, the locator of a claim was allowed but one hundred feet of territory along the vein."

With a precipitous hike in population comes a flock of purveyors eager to profit on supplying the influx. Before long, Buckskin Joe's main street hosted: "the theater, the Grand Hotel and several public houses, billiard halls, stores, saloons, stage office, post office, and the bank of Stansell, Bond & Harris."

Then one fine day, the stage delivered an exceptionally lovely young lady who quickly became the town's favorite hoofer. The besotted miners lined up outside Si Turner's saloon perfumed the air with aromas of soap, witch hazel, and bay rum—their atypical ablutions performed in honor of the newcomer with whom they could hardly wait to whirl around the dance floor.

Silver Heels, they called her, for the way the light glinted off her shiny, silver-filigreed shoes. Which undoubtedly rated notice while her admirers were mesmerized by glimpses of her comely ankles and flashes of a well-turned calf.

And law, that girl—she could dance. *Rocky Mountain Memories* columnist Frances Melrose cited a 1948 interview with Colonel Frank Mayer, a ninety-eight-year-old Fairplay resident and one-time U.S. Marshal at Buckskin Joe. Mayer claimed he saw Silver Heels alight from the stagecoach the day she came to town, adding, "I never seen a more beautiful interpretive dancer."

Silver Heels reportedly occupied a tidy cabin across the creek from the town proper. Although the majority of dance hall girls earned much of their living on the horizontal, rather than vertically, it's said "Aunt Martha," an older woman, the widow of a busted prospector, lived with her and saw to the dancer's care, feeding, and wardrobe.

A favorite pastime during daylight hours was picking wildflowers. The table in Silver Heels's cabin always had a bouquet in a tin cup for a centerpiece.

Some sources also attest that an unnamed protector, who feared for her virtue, walked her home from the saloon every night and slept on the stoop. Another mentions her falling in love with a gambler named Buck Wilson.

But it was the fateful arrival of a herd of sheep in the spring of 1861 that permanently etched Silver Heels's moniker in the annals of Colorado history.

The shepherds may have merely passed through town en route to greener pastures, or drove their lambchops on the hoof to the district to sell. In either case, it seems the townies didn't look askance at the lesions dotting the shepherds' faces until they'd pocketed the proceeds and moved on—or, in the greener-pastures version, someone discovered their smallpox-blistered corpses.

A half-century earlier, English physician Edward Jenner observed that milkmaids often contracted cowpox (a less fatal cousin of smallpox), but the contagion didn't develop into variola. Jenner then extracted fluid from a milkmaid's cowpox pustule and injected it into an eight-year-old boy. Six weeks later, the poor child was injected with fluid from a smallpox lesion. Lucky for him, the boy didn't develop symptoms.

From the experiment, Jenner coined the term *vaccine* from *vaca*, the Latin word for "cow." By 1800, approximately one hundred thousand people were vaccinated against smallpox worldwide. Unfortunately, that number didn't include the shepherds or any residents of Buckskin Joe.

An outflux of population occurred faster than folks had flooded into the mining district. Most of the women and children were evacuated to Denver City. (If infected, they could have spread the epidemic there.) Many of the miners stayed put, fearing claim-jumpers more than the deadly plague.

Telegrams begging for nurses were dispatched to Denver City, but no help was forthcoming. Seeing her dance hall swains begin to drop like lesioned flies, Silver Heels dug in her fancy shoes and refused to budge.

If she was wearing a mask when she came to town, one branch of the legend says it was to hide her smallpox scars, hence knew she was immune to the contagion. Whether a pure-hearted Samaritan or a past victim of the disease, she definitely did nurse the sick, cook for them, and wash their fever-fetid linens and clothing.

Such was all imported nurses could have done, had they answered the town's pleas for help. A medical book published two decades after Buckskin Joe's epidemic prescribes aconite and belladonna (both toxic in large doses), then, as symptoms progress, bryonia, opium, stramonium, tart-emetic, mercuris, arsenicum, and sulfur—by name alone, the palliatives likely as inclined toward mortal consequences as smallpox.

Though her patient load was enormous, Silver Heels was probably aware that the victims eyes must be bathed frequently with cold water, lest the lesions spread and leave survivors blinded in one or both eyes.

Crudely fashioned and misspelled signs were nailed to dozens of cabin doors. KEP AWAY. KWARNTEEN. SMALPOCKS. For those who couldn't write, or read, charcoal-drawn pictures of a skull-and-crossbones said it all.

Besides tending to the living, Silver Heels buried the dead. The still-healthy may have dug the graves, but it's debatable. The prospect of catching smallpox from victims (the majority shrouded in blankets) buried six feet under could have ranked self-preservation well above shoveling a final resting place for the dead.

Somewhere in town, there was surely a noxious bonfire fueled by the deceaseds' sheets, blankets, clothing—anything their victims owned that could be burned. It wasn't uncommon for homes of families wiped out by the disease to be reduced to ashes—sometimes with the bodies inside. The two things most people knew about smallpox was that it spread like wildfire, and that fire was the only guarantee against accidental contamination.

The legend diverts again in regard to the fate of Silver Heels. In one, about the time the epidemic waned, she fell ill and the now-immune miners nursed her back to health, though her lovely face was ravaged by pockmarks.

Realizing her beauty was her meal ticket, in appreciation for saving their lives, the men took up a collection amounting to five thousand dollars in coin and pouches of gold dust. Alas, the courier who delivered it found her cabin empty, save for an abandoned, silver-filigree shoe and a tin cup of wildflowers hurled into a dark corner.

The masked Silver Heels story is similar, in that the miners took up a collection and delivered it to her, but found the door open and her trademark shoes winking back in the center of the floor.

Or, she adopted the mask or a heavy veil to camouflage her scarred complexion and she and Buck Wilson both vanished from Buckskin Joe. Search parties fanned out in the surrounding hills and hollers to no avail.

Months later, a pock-faced man (Wilson?) and a heavily veiled woman were observed buying a marriage license in Granite, Colorado Territory. They exchanged vows in a room above a saloon, then left town.

Regional lore portends that for many years a man wandered down from the San Juan Mountains to a village outpost every six months or so to trade furs and gold dust for supplies. Besides food and necessities, he always bought several expensive silk gowns.

Over time, various folks were compelled to ask the nameless stranger why he bought dresses along with the requisite salt, coffee, beans, and bacon. His reply never varied. "For a beautiful woman," he'd say, then turn and set out for his homestead in the hills.

On one point all stories agree: After the epidemic was over, the beloved dance hall girl left Buckskin Joe without saying good-bye to a soul. Because her disappearance negated the collection they'd taken for her, the miners named the snowcapped mountain peak rising 13,835 feet (or 13,822—sources don't even agree on *that*) in the near distance Mount Silver Heels.

The legend doesn't end there, though. Every year or so, some swore they'd seen a veiled woman clutching a bouquet of wildflowers or would find roses decorating the graves of those who died during the scourge.

There would be flowers laid on the grave of Buck Wilson, Silver Heels's one true love, whom she couldn't save from the ravages of the disease.

Or, as Jeremy Agnew reported in a *Post-Empire* story published in November 1980, after driving to and exploring what little remains of the old boomtown and its cemetery:

> I thought I saw her straighten up and move over to the next grave . . . I strained my eyes through the dusk. She was dressed in what looked like a long, gray, loose dress . . . her face was obscured by . . . a gray hood. . . . It looked like she might have a veil over her face, as if hiding it from view.
>
> . . . I started to walk toward [her] . . . But I found I could never quite reach her . . . Through the gathering dusk it was hard to see anything except this ghostly figure drifting through the trees.

On May 12, 1954, the University of Denver Little Theater debuted a musical production titled *Silverheels*. Waldo Williams composed the music and Russell Porter, the libretto.

Frances Melrose's review said the songs had "the same kind of rollicking bounce to be found in *Oklahoma!*" and called one number, "There's Goin' to Be a Wedding," a real toe-tapper.

Later in Melrose's reminiscences about the play, Frank H. Ricketson Jr., at the time an "official of 20th Century Fox Studio," believed Silverheels was "surefire Broadway stage material."

Ricketson's enthusiasm was apparently not unanimous. Ensuing negotiations fell asunder, along with the musical's creators' dreams of hitting the big time.

Thus far, anyway. After all, whatever bits and fragments one chooses to assemble into a whole, the legend does make for a heck of a tale. And regardless of how tall a few variations might be, they're by no means near the elevation of the gorgeous snowy peak a cadre of grateful miners christened Mount Silver Heels a century and a half ago.

BIBLIOGRAPHY

Groh, George. "Doctors of the Frontier." *American Heritage*, April 1963.

Laurence, Frances. *Maverick Women.* Carpinteria, CA: Manifest Publications, 1998.

Luchetti, Cathy, and Carol Olwell. *Women of the West.* New York: Crown Publishers, 1982.

Reiter, Joan Swallow. *The Women.* New York: Time-Life Books, Inc., Revised, 1979.

Shirley, Gayle C. *More Than Petticoats: Remarkable Oregon Women.* Guilford, CT: Falcon Publishing, 1998.

Sovereigns of Themselves. Vol. I. Abridged Online Edition, compiled by M. Constance Guardino III, with Rev. Marilyn A. Riedel.

2. HARRIET HUBBARD AYER

Aldrich, Elizabeth. *From the Ballroom to Hell.* Evanston, IL: Northwestern University Press, 1991.

Ayer, Harriet Hubbard. *Harriet Hubbard Ayer's Book: A Complete and*

Authentic Treatise on the Laws of Health and Beauty. New York: New York Times Books, 1974.

Ayer, Margaret Hubbard, and Isabella Taves. *The Three Lives of Harriet Hubbard Ayer*. London: W. H. Allen, 1957.

Gould, George M., A. M., M. D. *A Pocket Medical Dictionary, Giving the Pronunciation and Definition of the Principal Words Used in Medicine and the Collateral Sciences*. Philadelphia: P. Blakiston's Son & Co., 1915.

Kroeger, Brooke. *Nellie Bly*. New York: Times Books/Random House, 1994.

Riordan, Teresa. *Inventing Beauty: A History of the Innovations That Have Made Us Beautiful*. New York: Broadway, 2004.

Sutherland, Daniel E. *The Expansion of Everyday Life, 1860–1876*. New York: Harper & Row, 1989.

Thomas, Rolla L. *The Eclectic Practice of Medicine*. Cincinnati: The Scudder Brothers Company, 1907.

3. MARTHA MUNGER BLACK

Adney, Tappan. *The Klondike Stampede*. Vancouver: UBC Press, 1994.

Backhouse, Frances. *Women of the Klondike*. North Vancouver: Whitecap Books, 1995.

Bassett, Isabel. *The Parlour Rebellion: Profiles in the Struggle for Women's Rights*. Toronto: McClelland and Stewart Limited, 1975.

Bell, Andrew. *History of Canada*. Vol. II. Montreal: Richard Worthington, 1866.

Berton, Pierre. *The Klondike Fever*. New York: Alfred A. Knopf, 1958.

Marks, Paula Mitchell. *Precious Dust: The American Gold Rush Era: 1848–1900.* New York: William Morrow, 1994.

Martin, Carol. *Martha Black: Gold Rush Pioneer.* Buffalo: Douglas & McIntyre, 1996.

O'Connor, Richard. *High Jinks on the Klondike.* New York: Bobbs-Merrill, 1954.

4. SARAH KNIGHT BORGINNIS BOWMAN

Fehrenbach, T. R. *Lone Star.* Washington, D.C.: American Legacy Press, 1983.

Hamilton, Nancy. *The Women Who Won the West.* New York: Avon Books, 1980.

Handbook of Texas Online. s.v., "Bowman, Sarah," http://www.tsha .utexas.edu/handbook/online/articles/BB/fbo3o.html (accessed June 3, 2005).

Reiter, Joan Swallow. *The Women.* New York: Time-Life Books, Inc., 1978.

Smith, Robert Barr. "Bighearted, Big-fisted and Just Plain Big, 'Great Western' Held Her Own on the Frontier." *Wild West Magazine.* August 1997.

Stevens, Autumn. *Wild Women.* Berkeley: Conari Press, 1992.

5. MARGARET "MOLLY" BROWN

Adams, Abby. *An Uncommon Scold.* New York: Simon & Schuster, 1989.

Caren, Eric, and Steve Goldman. *Extra: Titanic, the Story of the*

Disaster in the Newspapers of the Day. Edison, NJ: Castle Books, 1998.

Caughey, Bruce, and Dean Winstanley. *The Colorado Guide.* Golden, CO: Fulcrum Publishing, 1994.

Dorset, Phyllis Flanders. *The New Eldorado.* New York: Barnes & Noble, Inc., edition, 1994.

Iversen, Kristen. *Molly Brown: Unraveling the Myth.* Boulder, CO: Johnson Books, 1999.

Marks, Paula Mitchell. *Precious Dust.* New York: William Morrow, 1994.

Shirley, Gayle C. *More Than Petticoats: Remarkable Colorado Women.* Guilford, CT: The Globe Pequot Press, 2002.

6. NELLIE CASHMAN

Arizona Historical Society. Archived Brophy, Cashman Gray, Mazzanovich and Manes Collections. Tucson, Arizona.

Backhouse, Frances. *Women of the Klondike.* North Vancouver: Whitecap Books, 1995.

Brophy, Frank Cullen. "God and Nellie." *Alive,* October 1973.

Clum, John P. "Nellie Cashman." *Arizona Historical Review,* October 1931.

Ledbetter, Suzann. *Nellie Cashman: Prospector and Trailblazer.* El Paso: Texas Western Press, 1993.

Zanjani, Sally. *A Mine of Her Own.* Lincoln, NE: University of Nebraska Press, 1997.

7. LAURA FAIR

Kaynor, Fay Campbell. *Lapdogs and Bloomer Girls: The Life and Times of Lisle Lester (1837–1888)*. Glendale, CA: First Eve's Eye Press, 2001.

Stephens, Autumn. *Wild Women*. Berkeley: Conari Press, 1992.

Streeter, Holly. "The Sordid Trial of Laura D. Fair: Victorian Family Values." www.law.georgetown.edu/ghl/streeter.htm. 1995.

8. HENRIETTA GREEN

Brubaker, Paul W. "The Witch of Wall Street." *The Bread Basket*, no date cited.

Cottrell, Debbie Mauldin. *The Handbook of Texas Online*. University of Texas-Austin.

Ginger, Ray. *Age of Excess*. New York: Macmillan, 1965.

Grinder, Brian, M.D., and Dan Cooper, M.D. "Hetty Green: Legendary Wall Street Investor," *Museum of American Financial History*, 1996.

Ketchum, Richard M. "Faces from the Past—VI." *American Heritage*, April 1962.

McCabe, Marsha. "Setting Record Straight on Hetty Green." *The Sunday Standard Times* (New Bedford, MA), March 18, 2001.

Schoenberger, Chana R. "The Witch of Wall Street." *Forbes*, November 2004.

Van Doren, Charles (editor). *Webster's American Biographies*. Springfield, MA: G. & C. Merriam Company, 1975.

"Women in American History." *Encyclopedia Brittanica* online, copyright 1999.

Yohn, Susan M. "Crippled Capitalists: Gender Ideology, the In-scription of Economic Dependence and Female Entrepreneurs in Nineteenth Century America." Hofstra University (no date cited).

9. ELSA JANE GUERIN

Aldrich, Elizabeth. *From the Ballroom to Hell.* Evanston, IL: North-western University Press, 1991.

Guerin, Mrs. E. J. *Mountain Charley: Or the Adventures of Mrs. E.J. Guerin who was thirteen years in male attire.* Norman, OK: University of Oklahoma Press, 1968.

L'Amour, Angelique. *A Trail of Memories.* New York: Bantam Books, 1988.

Laurence, Frances. *Maverick Women.* Carpinteria, CA: Manifest Publications, 1998.

Reiter, Joan Swallow. *The Women.* New York: Time-Life Books, Inc., 1978.

Shirley, Gayle C. *More Than Petticoats: Remarkable Colorado Women.* Guilford, CT: The Globe Pequot Press, 2002.

Sutherland, Daniel E. *The Expansion of Everyday Life, 1860–1876.* New York: Harper & Row, 1989.

Wheeler, Keith. *The Railroaders.* New York: Time-Life Books, 1973.

10. FRANCES BENJAMIN JOHNSTON

Bearor, Karen. Review of *The Woman Behind the Lens*, by Bettina Berch. *NWSA Journal* 13 (2) (summer 2001): 157–60.

"A Capital Education." *American Heritage,* June 1972.

Daniel, Pete, and Raymond Smock. *A Talent for Detail.* New York: Harmony Books, 1974.

James, Jacqueline. "Uncle Tom? Not Booker T." *American Heritage,* August 1968.

Poole, Lynn and Gray Poole. *Men Who Pioneered Inventions.* New York: Dodd Mead & Company, 1969.

Ricchiardi, Sherry. "Getting the Picture." *American Journalism Review,* January 1998.

Stephens, Autumn. *Wild Women.* Berkeley: Conari Press, 1992.

Steinburg, Steven L. "George Grantham Bain: pioneer of news photography." In *The National Pastime.* Lincoln, NE: University of Nebraska Press, 2004.

Wicks, Frank. "Picture this: Scientist? Businessman? The inventor who popularized photography spent his fortune well." *Mechanical Engineering-CIME,* July 2004.

II. ADAH ISAACS MENKEN

Brown, Dee. *The Gentle Tamers.* New York: Bantam Books, 1958.

Dickson, Samuel. "Adah Isaacs Menken" segment from NBC-KPO/KNBC (now KNBR, San Francisco) radio series "This Is Your Home," circa 1950.

Falk, Bernard. *The Naked Lady.* London: Hutchinson & Co., 1952.

Huffaker, Clair. *Profiles of the American West.* New York: Pocket Books, 1976.

Ray, Grace Ernestine. *Wily Women of the West.* San Antonio, TX: Naylor Co., 1972.

Stephens, Autumn. *Wild Women.* Berkeley: Conari Press, 1992.

US-Israel.org/source/biography, "Adah Isaacs Menken," no author citation.

12. WILMA FRANCES MINOR, CLARA DeBOYER,
ANN RUTLEDGE

Clymer, Floyd. *Those Wonderful Old Automobiles.* New York: Bonanza Books, 1953.

Fehrenbacher, Don E. *Heroic Apocrypha.* "Lincoln's Lost Letters," Louis A. Warren Lincoln Library and Museum, 1979.

Laning, Edward. "Spoon River Revisited." *American Heritage,* June, 1971.

Luce, Henry R., editor. *TIME Capsule/1929.* New York: Time-Life Books, Inc., 1967.

Minor, Wilma Frances. "Lincoln the Lover," Parts I, II, III. *The Atlantic Monthly,* December 1928, January 1929.

Sommer, Robin Langley. *Great Cons & Con Artists.* Philadelphia: Courage Books/Running Press Book Publishers, 1994.

Walsh, John Evangelist. *The Shadows Rise.* Urbana, IL: University of Illinois Press, 1993.

Wilson, Douglas L. *Lincoln Before Washington.* Urbana, IL: University of Illinois Press, 1997.

13. ELISABET NEY

Crawford, Ann Fears, and Crystal Sassee Ragsdale. *Women in Texas.* Barnet, TX: Eakin Press, 1982.

Freligh, M., M.D. *Homeopathic Practice of Medicine*. New York: Charles T. Hurlburt, 1884.

Hansen, Harry, editor. *Texas: A Guide to the Lone Star State*. New York: Hastings House, 1969.

Reiter, Joan Swallow. *The Women*. New York: Time-Life Books, Inc., 1978.

Stephens, Autumn. *Wild Women*. Berkeley: Conari Press, 1992.

14. SARA PARTON (FANNY FERN)

"A purchase on goodness: Fanny Fern, Ruth Hall and fraught individualism." *Studies in American Fiction*, September 22, 2003.

Huebl-Naranjo, Linda. "From Peek-A-Boo to Sarcasm," Pt. 6 of 7. Contemporary Women's Issues Database, September 1, 1995.

Kaynor, Fay Campbell. *Lapdogs and Bloomer Girls*. Glendale, CA: First Eve's Eye Press, 2001.

Kelley, Mary. *Private Woman, Public Stage*. New York: Oxford University Press, 1984.

Warren, Joyce W. *Fanny Fern: An Independent Woman*. New Brunswick, NJ: Rutgers University Press, 1992.

Warren, Joyce W., editor. *Ruth Hall and Other Writings*. New Brunswick, NJ: Rutgers University Press, 1994.

White, Barbara A., contributing editor, "Fanny Fern (Sara Willis Parton) (1811–1872)." Houghton Mifflin Educational Division database.

Winokur, Jon. *Writers on Writing*. Philadelphia: Running Press, 1990.

15. LYDIA PINKHAM

Armstrong, David, and Elizabeth Metzger Armstrong. *The Great American Medicine Show*. New York: Prentice Hall, 1991.

Brodie, Janet Farrell. *Contraception and Abortion in 19th-Century America*. Ithaca, NY: Cornell University Press, 1994.

Burton, Jean. *Lydia Pinkham Is Her Name*. New York: Farrar, Straus and Company, 1949.

Carson, Gerald. "Sweet Extract of Hokum." *American Heritage*, June 1971.

Edwards, Bob, host. "Lydia E. Pinkham's Vegetable Compound," Morning Edition transcript, National Public Radio, February 20, 2001.

Holbrook, Stewart H. *The Golden Age of Quackery*. New York: The Macmillan Company, 1959.

Krochmal, Arnold, and Connie Krochmal. *A Field Guide to Medicinal Plants*. New York: Times Books, 1984.

Walsh, Nancy. "Studies Find Black Cohosh Eases Menopause Symptoms." *Family Practice News*, March 15, 2001.

Wilbur, C. Keith, M.D. *Revolutionary Medicine 1700–1800*. Chester, CT: The Globe Pequot Press, 1980.

16. MATTIE SILKS

Brodie, Janet Farrell. *Contraception and Abortion in 19th-Century America*. Ithaca, NY: Cornell University Press, 1994.

Dary, David. *Seeking Pleasure in the Old West*. New York: Alfred A. Knopf, 1995.

Dorset, Phyllis Flanders. *The New Eldorado*. New York: Barnes & Noble Books, 1994.

Dumas, Alan. "Dialing Into the Past; Old Phone Books Turn Into History at Hands of Retired Telecom Worker." *Denver Rocky Mountain News*. September 1, 1997.

Noel, Thomas J. *The City and the Saloon: Denver 1858–1916*. Lincoln, NE: University of Nebraska Press, 1982.

Pease, Marguerite Jenison, editor. *The Story of Illinois*. Chicago: University of Chicago Press, 1967.

Reiter, Joan Swallow. *The Women*. New York: Time-Life Books, Inc., 1978.

Seagraves, Anne. *Soiled Doves: Prostitution in the Early West*. Hayden, ID: Wesanne Publications, 1994.

Webb, James R. "Pistols for Two . . . Coffee for One." *American Heritage*, February 1975.

17. SILVER HEELS

Agnew, Jeremy. "They Called Her Silverheels." *Post-Empire*, November 1980.

Benson, Maxine. *1001 Colorado Place Names*. Lawrence, KS: University Press of Kansas, 1994.

Dorsett, Phyllis Flanders. *The New Eldorado*. New York: Barnes & Noble Books, 1994.

Freligh, M., M.D. *Homeopathic Practice of Medicine*. New York: Charles T. Hurlburt, 1884.

"Ghosts of Park County; Buckskin Joe," http://members.aol.com/JKA80122/park.html.

Harley, William B. "Silver Heels." *True Western Adventure,* December 1958.

"The History of Smallpox." About.com

McGrath, Maria Davies. "The Real Pioneers of Colorado." Vol. Two, CWA Project No. 551.

Melrose, Frances. "Musical 'Silverheels' Turned Heads in '54." *Rocky Mountain News,* August 9, 1998.

Melrose, Frances. "Silverheels lives in mining camp legends." Rocky Mountain Memories (column), *Rocky Mountain News,* November 6, 1983.

"Reminiscences of Old Buckskin." *Denver Daily Tribune,* June 25, 1879.